Praise for *When We Were Gods*

"The writing is professional, the first person approach direct, un-self-conscious and uncluttered. I was interested in reading more—that doesn't happen often."
- JOHN ANTHONY WEST, AUTHOR, *SERPENT IN THE SKY: THE HIGH WISDOM OF ANCIENT EGYPT*, www.jawest.net

"We should not underestimate the discrete, immeasurable influences of nature. In *When We Were Gods,* Carole Chapman unfolds a personal quest and vision that is not only entertaining, but inspirational."
- CHRISTOPHER DUNN, AUTHOR, *THE GIZA POWER PLANT*, www.gizapower.com

"Carol Chapman listened to dreams that came from her innermost consciousness. Encompassing the Fifth Root Race, the Great Pyramid of Giza and Atlantis, she has written a history of the soul on Earth. Based on her own experiences of finding her inner roots, Carole presents a blueprint for a new generation to find meaning and direction for their lives and become the Golden Ones. In an age when the 'God' gene has been identified within the human genome, *When We Were Gods* can lead its readers to be like gods again."
- DANIEL KOLOS, EGYPTOLOGIST, POET, CO-AUTHOR,
  THE NAME OF THE DEAD: TUTANKHAMUN TRANSLATED,
  www.bmts.com/~damilos

"A must-read book, *When We Were Gods* explores both the history of our souls and our future evolution, providing an insightful view of today's children, many of them Indigos, who will awaken to their destiny and become stepping-stones to the Fifth Root Race."
- MARY ANN CARR, M.Ed., SPECIALIST IN GIFTED EDUCATION,
  AUTHOR, *ONE HOUR MYSTERIES*

More Praise for *When We Were Gods*

"An incredibly interesting book, beautifully written. It reminds me of Shirley MacLaine's *The Camino*—about the time before we had bodies, when the sexes weren't yet separated."
- SUSAN LENDVAY, ASSOCIATE EDITOR, *VENTURE INWARD*, THE MEMBERSHIP MAGAZINE OF EDGAR CAYCE'S A.R.E., www.edgarcayce.org

"*When We Were Gods* is a thought-provoking first-person account of Carole Chapman's hypnotic exploration of apparent and ancient past life memories of a most incredible nature—'memories' that cited an extraterrestrial origin, as well as a past life, a strange root race, and the superior and mysterious technology of Atlantis, with a thing called 'snake travel' (would quantum physicists call it a 'wormhole'?) thrown into the mix. What you have is a fascinating autobiographical accounting of Carole's memories, how she initially reacted to them and eventually came to deal with them, and the efforts and lengths to which she undertook to try and objectively confirm the truth of their reality—a journey and search that took her to Central America and Egypt. What she learned challenges conventional science and understanding, and it may take the emerging science of theoretical quantum physics to eventually confirm the actual truth of her bewildering 'memories.' A genuinely intriguing and thought-provoking book!"
- BRENT RAYNES, EDITOR, *ALTERNATE PERCEPTIONS*, AUTHOR, *VISITORS FROM HIDDEN REALMS*, www.mysterious-america.net

"A new wave of spiritual seeking is sweeping the planet. Many of the enlightened ones, such as Carole Chapman, communicate the message so that others can pay attention to their intuition and remember that which we once knew. *When We Were Gods* should be experienced by everyone searching to reach a higher level."
- JOE SAITTA, VICE PRESIDENT (RET.), FOX TELEVISION AFFILIATE NEWS

More Praise for *When We Were Gods*

" . . . stimulating, thought-provoking, well-written and hopeful."
- BLANCHE HERRING SHARF, *CHESAPEAKE STYLE*

"It reads like a mystery, and the explanations of ancient events felt real to me, even though I'm new to some of the concepts mentioned. I like that the chapters got to the point without getting too contemplative."
- LEE ANN DAIL, VIRGINIA, USA

"This book is incredible. The information that came in to the author was information I was looking for—of how the soul came to Earth, about Atlantis, and the future. It's very spiritual but also very logical—how things work and why things work."
- VERNA JUNIPER, ONTARIO, CANADA

"I cannot imagine the courage it took to write this book . . . Slowly we realize that we are not simply enjoying a dramatic adventure . . . this is a sacred testimony that we have been called to hear! It is an epistle of enlightened facts, divinely inspired and beautifully written, providing astounding insights into our world's fundamental mysteries and our own deepest knowledge."
- RICKI BAER, PSY.D., NORTH CAROLINA, USA

"This is a POWERFUL book! Part adventure story and suspense mystery, full of Biblical references and New Age insights, it will appeal to many minds. We are kept riveted to our seats. As *When We Were Gods* unfolds, we become aware that Carole's story is OUR story. "The History of the Soul" in the earth plane and beyond."
- NANCY J. OATES, CONNECTICUT, USA

More Praise for *When We Were Gods*

"Carole's experience is both inspiring and thought-provoking. As long as we seek the truth about why we are here, it seems we have a chance to bring about changes that are needed not only for our own benefit but for the benefit of all life."
- JOYCE F. KELLER, NEBRASKA, USA

"Her travel to Mayan ruins in the Yucatan, where she finds confirmation of her reasons of existence would send chills down your back."
- EVELYN FREEMAN, VIRGINIA, USA

"I urge you to read this book. It's a fun read and adds some awesome suggestions and insights to well known information. From A Course in Miracles to Ramtha, from ancient Aramaic scripture to current quantum physics, this information is available."
- KAREN A. RANDALL, CONNECTICUT, USA

"I really enjoyed reading [*the book*]. I took it to the hospital with me to read. I didn't put it down for a minute. It answered some questions that I have been seeking answers to."
- PAULETTE CLASS, ILLINOIS, USA

"The author's visions help to give understanding to the human condition leading to the Biblical story and, like the Biblical story, give hope for a better world."
- THE REV. LOUISE AIKMAN, ONTARIO, CANADA

"I love the part about the frog in the tower—how the frog could feel the electromagnetic field in its body."
- BOB SADLER, VIRGINIA, USA

When We Were

GODS

Insights on Atlantis, Past Lives, Angelic Beings of Light, and Spiritual Awakening

by Carole Chapman

with
23 Images
a Bibliography
an Index
and
Seven Articles

The Second Revised Edition of
The Golden Ones: From Atlantis to a New World

SunTopaz LLC
Foster, VA

When We Were Gods:
Insights on Atlantis, Past Lives, Angelic Beings of Light, and Spiritual Awakening

by Carole Chapman

Published by: SunTopaz LLC, PO Box 123, Foster, VA 23056
www.SunTopaz.com

Second Revised Edition of *The Golden Ones: From Atlantis to a New World*
First Edition © 2000

Printed in the United States of America.

The article, "Arcturus is Home" is reprinted with permission from FATE Magazine.

Disclaimer
The information within these pages is not meant to be used as professional advice of any kind. It is merely meant to provide information and entertainment. If you suffer with obesity or depression or any other ailment, you should seek a qualified medical practitioner.

Library of Congress Control Number: 2005906373

Library of Congress Cataloging-in-Publication Data
Chapman, Carole
        When we were gods: insights on Atlantis, past lives, angelic beings of light and spiritual awakening / Carole Chapman; foreword by Lynn Sparrow

Includes bibliographical references and index
ISBN: 0-9754691-1-8

1. New age movement. 2. Atlantis. 3. Hypnotism—Case studies. 4. Inspirational stories. 5. Reincarnation. 6. Spiritual life. I. Title. II. Chapman, Carole.

Cover design © 2005 Clair Balsley
Cover and internal photographs © 2004 Carole Chapman
Photo of the author © 2004 Clair Balsley
This edition edited by Clair Balsley

Dedicated to My Family

Contents

Acknowledgements

This book would not have been possible without the Love and Light, common to all of us, that fires the universe—bits of which manifested through my Higher Self to reveal the information that is the basis of this book. From the depth of my being, thank you.

In addition, I am grateful for the magnificent Light Beings who have made themselves available to little droplets of Light such as myself: those known in the Western culture as Christ, Gabriel, and Michael, members of the Brotherhood, who are so concerned with our freedom from the dark. Thank you for being mindful of us. And, lest I forget the 13th fairy, I acknowledge that force, also made by the Creator, known as Lucifer, who tempts us that we may be strengthened.

To Pan and the nature kingdom: Greetings! Thank you for making my world exist and for participating in the great experiment to turn our wills back to the Creator. I also appreciate that you came to me and that you are so willing to cooperate with us.

Thank you, also, to all those whose Higher Selves brought them and will bring them to this information. May I be a channel of blessings to you. And may you be awakened to the truth of who we really are, what we are really doing here, and where we are really going.

A very special thank you for the support, financial and emotional, from my husband John, the man of my dreams, the catalyst and my stability through these awakenings.

I am especially appreciative of all the help I received from my daughter Clair Catherine Balsley, whose wonderful spirit supported and believed in me through the fear and the exhilaration. You listened to me, made wonderful suggestions, and read the final manuscript, correcting many mistakes and reducing my long-windedness. Thank you.

Thanks also to Miriam Hope Balsley, my youngest daughter, for her very succinct comments that helped me to clarify the direction of my writing. In addition, I appreciate the talks with my son, Adam Jason Balsley, and my daughter-in-law, Cher Elizabeth Balsley. All of my children were so helpful in showing me the topics that were of interest to young people.

Thanks to Lynn Sparrow, whose humanity and expertise were pivotal throughout the hypnosis sessions, and whose professional and succinct foreword introduces the book with such grace.

To Peggy Rose Day, the editor meant to midwife this work. So many e-mails and snail mails passed between our desks—every word of advice a flower of encouragement. Through her gentle hands flows an abiding faith.

For the cover photo I am indebted to my model, Adam Jason Balsley, my son, who awoke before dawn, drove with me in the dark, and waited in the cool breeze off the ocean for the sun to break through the horizon. Thank you for sharing that magical moment with me and so patiently posing while I went through rolls and rolls of film. Thanks also to Photo Imaging in Newport News, Virginia, especially Jeffrey, Jim, Anne, and Mike (and also Jimmy for his excellent advice); to Camera City in Hampton, Virginia, and especially Lynn Allred and to Cindy Perry at Winn Dixie's One Hour Photo in Gloucester, Virginia. In addition, I appreciate all the support I've received for furthering my talents in photography from Gary Price, Cam Martin, Elaine Camhi, Lee Battaglia, David Heath, and Jergen Lutz. Thank you also to Joseph Moore for giving so generously of his personal time showing me how to make the web site, and to Jenn Ferry for her help with the web site.

Acknowledgements

Special thanks to my Mom and Dad, Bill and Leona Petrachenko, for making my life possible—my pretty little Mom for her enduring support of my creativity and my Dad for challenging my mind. Thanks to my brother Bill Petrachenko for our many long talks on things philosophical; my sister Sheila Petrachenko for sharing my life; and my brother Tom Petrachenko for brightening my life with his wonderful sense of humor. Also thanks to my step-son, Sean David Balsley, who was the first to teach me about remembering when he was a young boy learning how to swim.

There are so many more: Lore Aloro, who believed in me; A. Robert Smith, for his writing expertise, sound advice, and willingness to publish my first article on the Fifth Root Race in *Venture Inward*; Dr. C. Louise Kirk, for her encouragement and for the adjustments that made possible my long hours at the computer; Marian Jones, for her writing expertise and friendship; Joseph Dunn, A.R.E. Press editor, for his encouragement; the late J. Everett Irion for his wisdom and the 40-day prayer; and the Rev. Louise Aikman for encouraging me to use my psychic talents.

Thank you to my dear friend Celeste Kennedy for her abiding friendship; Kathy Bishop, for believing in and loving me for all these years; Nancy Ennis, who knew when we were seven years old that we were going to be writers; Peggy Joyce Smith, my early-morning walking and "God is greater" buddy; Janet Sheldon, my first fan; Melissa Jager, for long hours talking into the night; Thelma Lucas and Carole, for their joyful spirit; Sam Reinke for sharing his information and his joyous singing; Laurel Mellin, creator of The Solution, from whom I finally learned how to lose weight without dieting just as I finished the manuscript; Deanne Duvall, my Solution provider, for her warmth and support; and my Solution Group members for their encouragement.

Thanks also to Margaret Hunt, Marny Skora, Roger Hathaway and Richard Weeks for their support in encouraging me to approach the man of my dreams, and also Rick Hopson, John's dark-haired friend, who did so much to help John and me get together. In addition, a hearty thanks for Edgar Cayce and the Association for Research and Enlightenment that preserves his psychic readings—and especially their Search for God Study Groups, where I learned how to work with dreams, pray, meditate, and trust the God within. Thanks, too, for the many librarians who helped me, especially Jackie in Yorktown, Nancy Dwoyer and Mary B. in Gloucester, and Curly Diggs Lane at the A.R.E.

For all those I will suddenly remember and wish I had included in this acknowledgment *after* the book has been printed: Thank you for helping, inspiring, hearing, and encouraging me.

In conclusion, again I not only acknowledge my Source but also, in humble appreciation, praise and thanks from the depths of my being, I thank the Light Force, once known as Amilius and also Emmanuel, my Teacher, my Advocate, my Friend, for working with that small spark that is me.

Foreword

The narrative you are about to enjoy may be unlike anything else you have read. Part autobiography, part spiritual philosophy, part adventure story, part personal growth and self-help manual, part revelation of things unseen to the physical eye, it defies categorization. But whatever the genre one might choose to place it in, *When We Were Gods* is sure to stimulate the thinking and personal exploration of anyone who likes to be stretched; anyone who ponders the mysteries of life; and—above all—anyone who seeks a firmer grasp of the ultimate meaning in the universe.

While it is the story of one individual's quest for wholeness through inner work, *When We Were Gods* is also an amazing journey through our collective history. You will go back to "before the beginning," before we even inhabited flesh bodies, and experience the coming of the human race with the detail and directness that only a first-person account can give. The grand epochs of Atlantis and Egypt will take new meaning in the context of one soul's descent into materiality. You will look through the future-directed telescope of the author's altered state to see our ascent to new levels of spiritually-based existence in not-too-distant tomorrows. And along the way, you will be continually challenged to expand your notion of the here-and-now, as the writer's scope of revelatory experience arises from an ongoing interplay of dimensions and beings and forces that comprise the greater cosmos.

Yet this book is not primarily a history or a metaphysical treatise. It is a call to each of us to explore the vast, untapped memory and wisdom of the soul mind—both to meet the challenges of today and to more fully realize the potential of what it means to be a spiritual being in a three-dimensional world.

I first met the author when she came to me to do what we both expected to be fairly routine hypnotherapy for weight control. It soon became clear that something much deeper, something more germane to the story of us all, was seizing the opportunity to emerge. Often I sat, spellbound, as "slice of life" vignettes of history emerged via memories of lives in such diverse places as Atlantis, Egypt, First Century Palestine, the African jungle, revolutionary-era France and the pre-Civil-War American south. Then, just when I would think we were doing a textbook model past-life regression, Carole would move with what appeared to be effortless ease through some of the most profound aspects of theological or metaphysical thought and then back again to eminently practical advice for her health or her career or her eyesight! The seamless weave of the personal, transpersonal, and historical significance of these sessions was fascinating.

This, I think, is one of the attractions of the narrative that has developed from that hypnotic work, which spanned approximately three years. As I read the manuscript for *When We Were Gods*, I had the rare opportunity to take a broad view of an entire series of hypnosis sessions. And as I did, I was astounded at the amount, variety and depth of information, insight, and healing that is available to one who is ready to make a committed search to find it. From there, I realized that Carole's account highlights some of the most important themes for spiritual seekers of these times. These are themes that I have observed over and over again in working with clients, but previously they always appeared piecemeal. In this volume, you will see them exemplified within a single narrative that has all the flow of a unified story. To highlight these themes, I list them here for the reader's consideration:

The cosmic is best comprehended when seen through the lens of the personal. Theories and mythologies and teleologies can be cold and distant things. Even when we find them fascinating, they are often far removed from the everyday life concerns that occupy a more prominent place in our awareness. Increasingly, however, people are finding that what they thought were ordinary, personal concerns are the doorway to something larger and ultimately far more soul-satisfying than they had originally expected. In short, many of today's hypnotherapy clients are finding that the solving of a personal problem is inextricably linked with finding a deeper level of meaning to life and its challenges. Carole's story illustrates this theme magnificently.

People are developing increasing contact, rapport, and communication with the unconscious and with higher levels of awareness. Perhaps one of the questions uppermost in the minds of many readers of *When We Were Gods* will be "Can anyone do this? Can anyone enter hypnosis and go back to the beginning of time? Or move into levels of direct communication with angelic beings and Christ Himself?" My response to that question, from the perspective of the hypnotherapist's chair, is: Theoretically, yes; practically, no. Even the great American seer Edgar Cayce insisted that anyone could do what he did, yet only a few have seemed to be able to in fact fulfill that promise. Part of the ability may lie in the cumulative experience of many incarnations. But far more important are the ideals, purposes, and commitment level of the seeker. From the start, I was impressed with Carole's clarity of ideal and commitment of purpose, as well as her willingness to trust the flow rather than continually turn it off with second-guessing. It was always clear that her heart and soul were fully engaged in the process. And, perhaps equally important, she worked conscientiously with application of whatever she learned, session-by-session. Under such conditions, the potential for personal revelation is enormous, compared to what most of us ever bother to experience.

Expectations of the Third Millennium offer a mix of hopefulness and daunting challenge. While there are many different articulations of what might be called "prophetic" views of the time we have just entered, this blending of hope and dread seems to be the most characteristic feature. It is clear that the birth pangs of the long-awaited "new age" are objects of trepidation to many of us, yet the hope of what we can experience on the other side of the birth canal is a powerful motivator. A trend that I have noticed throughout the preceding decade is for people to come to hypnotherapy with an awareness that it is time to take care of unfinished business that has long been put off. People are realizing—often without knowing that others are realizing it too—that now is the time to get rid of the last baggage that would weigh them down. There is a sense of getting ready, being prepared. But for that preparation to be carried to completion, most of us need a sustaining vision of why it is important to do so. Many of my clients, though intuiting that such completion of unfinished business is no longer an option and has now become a necessity, are nonetheless not exactly sure what they are preparing for. The coming of the Golden Ones, the Fifth Root Race, which Carole describes with such unaffected clarity, leaves one with a golden hope for these times.

As I came to the end of the manuscript, I felt wonderfully buoyed up with the realization that we are embarking on the next level of our collective journey. Many are being given essentially the same message in our individual frameworks. With that came the knowledge that, stresses and uncertainties notwithstanding, it is a good time to be in the Earth.

Lynn Sparrow
January 2000
Author, *Reincarnation: Claiming the Past, Creating Your Future*

Author's Note

This book is written for the sincere ones. It is time for them to awaken. These are the people who, in Atlantis, were given or took upon themselves the task of preparing the Earth for a new Golden Age—the thousand years of peace on Earth. These, the Golden Ones, are here now, through reincarnation, ready and waiting to be awakened.

*   *   *

THE TIME IS NOW.
AWAKEN!

This is the way I was told to start this book. To the best of my ability, I have tried to honor the information that has come to me whether from the God within or telepathic beings.

This includes my marriage, because I first met my husband in a dream that told me he was the man I should marry. It was very hard for me to approach him when I first saw him in my waking life. But I did my best, and we have now been married for six years.

In the same way, I have done my best to be true to the directive in my hypnosis sessions to write a book—or in some way inform as many people as possible—of the advent of the Fifth Root Race and the history of the soul on Earth. Much of it is very controversial to me, but I have done my best to recount the information to you with as little bias as possible.

Except that occasionally words or phrases have been deleted to clarify the meaning, all the dialogue from the hypnosis sessions is copied verbatim from tapes. However, some of the ideas do not necessarily reflect my personal beliefs or opinions.

For example, I refer to archangels and Satan even though the religion of my childhood did not emphasize a celestial hierarchy. Nonetheless, on a recent trip to France, I was surprised to discover that there are tapestries, cathedrals, and even a medieval monastery at Mont St. Michele devoted to the archangels and the Apocalypse. I learned that the celestial hierarchy is a very strong part of the Roman Catholic Church.

In addition, during the time I was receiving information about the history of the soul on Earth, I was visited by an otherworldly being who I believe was Pan, Lord of the Wilderness. I have never before nor since had such an experience. When Pan talked to me, he suggested prayers that name Allah. I do not call God "Allah"; however, I have written it as it came to me.

In one session I refer to the lotus flower. I understand that the Buddha is often depicted as sitting on a lotus. Again, my conscious understanding of the lotus—and Buddhism—is very limited, but because it came up in the hypnosis, I have written it so.

There are also many other items, names, and concepts that came up, for example, the Brotherhood, about which I consciously know very little. Nonetheless, I have written what I saw and heard.

Although the words from the hypnosis sessions are copied verbatim, the dialogues between my daughter Clair and me are not exact. Their content represents various discussions I have had with her and my other two children, Adam and Miriam, as well as my daughter-in-law Cher.

The information within these pages is being presented to you with a healthy skepticism. It is a true story, but I make no claims that the information is truth. Nonetheless, I have researched other sources, such as the mythology of the Maya and the Hopi Nation, the Hindu religion as well as the readings of the psychic Edgar Cayce, the insights of the mystic Madame Helene Petrovna Blavat-

Author's Note

sky, and the knowledge of the clairvoyant Rudolf Steiner. I find that there is a correlation between the information in the hypnosis sessions and these other sources.

In addition, the information is meant to be helpful. I hope there is nothing in it that suggests anything but actions and concepts that are for the greater good of all. If some of it is threatening because it challenges accepted beliefs, know that it challenged me too. That is why I say, please read this with a healthy skepticism.

Author's Note to the Second Revised Edition

This second revised edition of *The Golden Ones* is called *When We Were Gods*. I chose to change the title because the new title is the original working title and goes better with the cover picture.

All along I had wanted to include photographs in the book. After all, I am a photojournalist by profession. The chapter on my travels in Yucatan especially required photographs to illustrate the information I conveyed. I feel happy that I was able to include 23 photographs in this edition.

There are also the wonderful photographs of the giant sunflowers and peppers that grew after the first edition of the book had gone to the printer. Pan, Lord of the Wilderness, had asked me to include a message in the book. The main impetus of his message was that nature had the power to clean up the Earth for mankind. I believe my fantastic garden, with peppers the size of squashes and 14-foot tall sunflowers resulted from my cooperation with Pan to include his message in the book. I believe it was Pan's way of showing what nature could do. I also want to thank my son, Adam Balsley and his wife, Cher Balsley, as well as my daughter Miriam Balsley for their input on the design of gorgeous cover of *When We Were Gods*.

Thanks also to Andrew Honigman, Associate Editor at *FATE Magazine*, for giving me the permission to reprint my article, "Arcturus is Home," in its entirety in the "Articles" section of this book. I also appreciate that *FATE Magazine* offered to publish the article in the first place. It's a great magazine.

Likewise, my thanks goes out to the editors of the following publications: *Alternate Perceptions, Circle Magazine, Dream Network, Venture Inward,* and *Whole Life Times,* for so graciously publishing my articles and photographs in their fantastic magazines.

In this edition, I want to also acknowledge all the wonderful support I've received from the many people who've heard me speak on the lecture circuit or on the radio. Because of their encouragement, personal stories, and by sharing their own experiences, I no longer feel so strange about my memories as a newcomer in the Earth, through the root races, and in Atlantis.

I especially want to thank Toni Romano, head of the Regional Outreach Department at Edgar Cayce's A.R.E. and the many regional coordinators in Chicago, Houston, New Jersey, New York City, and Seattle in the United States, and Vancouver, British Columbia and London, Ontario at Edgar Cayce Canada that hosted my seminars and weekend retreats. In addition, I extend my gratitude to Melinda Sharpe in Connecticut, Karen Randall in Rhode Island, and Susan Gale at A Place of Light in Massachusetts who organized A.R.E.-associated events.

Thanks also to Dean and Mary Hardy for inviting me to speak at the Temple of Sakkara annual weekend retreat in Michigan. In addition, I appreciate the lovely events organized by Louise Aikman, Verna Juniper, and Jocelyn Desautel in Southern Ontario, Canada, and also the events in Alaska organized by Skye High of the Ancient Teachings of the Masters Center. I also want to thank the many other people—the organizers and the volunteers— that made my events possible in the United States and Canada.

It has meant so much to me to be received so warmly and enthusiastically.

When We Were Gods

Part I:

When We Were

Gods

1

The Man of My Dreams

Have you ever had a dream that changed your life? Have you ever had a dream come true?

Everyone says they want to find the man or woman of their dreams. But what if it happened to you? What if you dreamt of a stranger you were supposed to marry—and then saw that person the next day? What would you do? Would you go up to them and say, "I just dreamt I'm supposed to marry you?" Or would you wait and watch, wondering what kind of person you had dreamt about?

I had the dream about five months after starting a job as photojournalist at NASA Langley Research Center in Hampton, Virginia. My photographs of aircraft and spaceship models, lasers and research planes, test pilots, astronauts, and scientists were being published all over the nation and internationally. My articles appeared in NASA publications. It was an exciting time in my life.

The dream had come the night after my last date with a man who had asked me to marry him. I had declined. This was not easy to do because the man was a millionaire, and I was a single mom with three almost-college-age youngsters.

Little did I know that the dream was just the beginning.

Little did I realize that I had just begun an amazing spiritual journey into the unknown, and I was about to unravel one of the deepest mysteries of who we really are. The morning I awoke from that dream, I had no idea that something much greater than myself had been set in motion and my life would forever be changed.

At the time, the children and I lived in a little house on a street adjacent to the Chesapeake Bay. Among the four of us, we shared one bed: I slept on the mattress, the girls used the box spring, and my son spent his nights on blankets piled on the wooden floor.

When the children and I had moved to Virginia Beach from Phoenix, we could bring only what we could fit into our old 1970 three-quarter-ton Ford window van. After we packed our clothes, dishes, pots, books, typewriter, stereo, toys, and my camera, there was no room for any furniture.

Our most precious passengers were our little terripoo dog, Muffin, and our four cats. We couldn't leave our beloved pets in Phoenix because they were a part of our family, and they gave us a sense of home no matter where we were or what happened to us.

My new job in Virginia, with a NASA contractor, paid enough for food, clothing, and school supplies, but we had to find our furniture on the side of the road on bulk garbage days.

It had not been easy to say "no" to my millionaire friend. He had taken me to lovely waterfront homes where he wanted us to live. How I missed having a nice home! We had had to leave Phoenix because our four-bedroom house with the in-ground pool had been foreclosed on when the children's father didn't pay child support for two years.

However, although we appeared to be destitute during those terrible years, our struggle to survive had brought us together as a family. The children and I had learned to trust and depend on each other. "One for all, and all for one," we used to say.

We found that, over and over again, things would work out. For example, when I went back to school to get my degree, one of my fellow students happened to be a mechanic who insisted on repairing my old vehicle—in the parking lot of Phoenix College. I typed his papers in return.

It was as if the children and I were in spiritual training.

My ex-husband had done me a favor, because when he threw me out of his life, I landed in God's arms.

When our air conditioning broke, we had to sleep on lawn chairs on the patio around the pool. As we fell asleep, the whole sky would be open above us. Sometimes we'd see a plane or a satellite traveling among the stars. Other times, there'd be heat lightning coloring the mountains that surrounded the valley. It was heavenly to slumber with a breeze fanning our sleeping bodies.

I'd come to appreciate even the smallest things—like being cool enough to sleep. The beauty and tranquility of the night sky will remain forever deep in my bones. I remember those nights under the stars, my children beside me, our dog and cats nearby, as one of the happiest times in my life. There is a remarkable peace to appreciating even the smallest things.

It was a time when I was closest to God, a time when it was easy to end each day with a prayer of thanksgiving: thanks that we had shelter for one more night, thanks that we had food for one more day, thanks that we had each other, and thanks that God's world resounded with beauty, drama, and peace—a peace that passed understanding.

Therefore, although it would have seemed as if the millionaire was a gift from heaven for all the years we had gone without even the necessities of life, the children and I were not really as needy as we appeared to be. We had immense faith that we could triumph over anything.

So I could not say "yes," because I did not love the man, although I admired and respected him. I did not want another marriage like the first. I wanted a soul mate—a twin soul.

With the wisdom of hindsight, I suppose the dream telling me the man I should marry came because I had kept to my ideals and resisted being swayed by the temptation of living well financially. I was holding out for love.

The entry in my dream journal was dated March 28, 1990. The first part of the dream was about the actor "Godunov," who played the husband destined to marry the single mother in the movie

Witness. In the dream, Godunov had this "high up" house that he had designed, a black lab-type dog, and a dark-haired male friend with a dark-haired wife. There was a satellite that represented someone's work.

In the next part of the dream, I saw a stage. In the spotlight center-stage, stood a tall, husky man with reddish-blonde hair standing with his back to me. As if on a turntable, he slowly rotated until he was facing me. I liked how he looked. He smiled a soft smile at me.

When I awoke, I assumed that my dream was telling me I had made the right choice in not marrying the millionaire. There was someone better out there for me, the proverbial plenty of fish in the sea, represented by the man in the second part of the dream.

I'd been keeping a dream journal for years and knew that dreams sometimes used words cleverly. In this case, "Godunov" sounded like and probably meant "good enough." Therefore, my unconscious most likely was telling me that somewhere out there was a man who might not be a millionaire but who was, nonetheless, "good enough" for me.

It never occurred to me that the man in the dream was a real person I was about to encounter.

You can imagine my astonishment when I walked down the cafeteria aisle next lunch hour, tray in hand, and I saw a man standing with his back to me filling his glass at the water fountain. I had been scanning the tables, looking for the friends who usually ate lunch with me. Searching for a familiar face, I was surprised to discover that this man at the water fountain looked like someone I had met before. He was a big man with a broad back and was wearing an orange-brown corduroy jacket which set off his reddish-blonde hair. As I walked by, my eyes at the level of his elbow, I glanced up at his face. It was the man in my dream! And I found him wildly attractive!

My heart pounded madly. I almost dropped my tray. I wanted to shout, "What were you doing in my dream last night?" But instead, I thought, "Hold onto your tray!" I was afraid I might faint. It took all my concentration to act normal in this cafeteria of hundreds of people.

I turned away, not wanting to stare. My breath came in short, quick bursts. I could feel my face redden and little beads of perspiration appeared around my mouth.

I didn't know what to do.

There are no etiquette manuals describing the proper behavior upon meeting the man of your dreams. There are no talk shows bringing dreamer together with dreamee. There are no articles in women's magazines telling how various people handled their first encounter with a man they'd just dreamt was their future husband.

I found my lunch friends and sat down, hoping my heartbeat couldn't be heard in the next county.

"Carole, what's wrong?" said one of my friends. "You look like you've seen a ghost."

"Uh, low blood sugar I guess." I didn't know what to say. And so I said nothing more about it, talking about anything and everything else—yet all the while looking over to where he sat. The only clue to my state of mind was a slight tremor in my hands. I felt like a young girl in the high school cafeteria.

When I got home that evening, I wrote in my dream journal: Just saw the man in my dream. He has a mustache and is chubbier—but nice. Looked at his hands—no ring.

You would think that now that I had found him, we would soon be living happily ever after. Sorry, this is a true story, not a fairy tale.

To begin, I was afraid. What did this mean, literally meeting the man of my dreams? What was going to happen to me if we got together? Was I in the grip of some kind of destiny?

For the next several weeks I watched him in the cafeteria, wondering what kind of man I had dreamt about. Was he a research scientist, an engineer who worked in the wind tunnels, an inventor, a technician, a test pilot, or support crew for our research aircraft? He often sat with work buddies, laughing and telling stories among themselves.

I kept waiting for him to recognize me, to be drawn inextricably toward me. Certainly, if he was the one I was destined to marry, wouldn't he be out there looking for me also? Shouldn't he feel my presence nearby? But he seemed totally oblivious to my existence.

The trouble with dreaming about the man I was supposed to marry was that he hadn't dreamt about me!

Time went by, and I became more and more reluctant to approach Mr. Good Enough, the Man of my Dreams. I consoled myself that he probably wasn't the right one. Likely all the details—the house, the dog, the best friend and the satellite—were probably false, and this man was probably a lucky look-alike. Maybe I had unknowingly seen him in the cafeteria before, and my unconscious had put him in my dream. In any case, I didn't want to appear a fool by approaching him.

I began to think that the dream had been a strange anomaly—perhaps just an indication that dreams can be real. In any case, I didn't see him again. Always mindful of my figure, I began eating at my desk and walking during lunch hour. Although I often had to take photographs in many of the more than 40 facilities throughout the Center, our paths never crossed. I never had to interview him or work with him during a press conference. Eventually I totally forgot about the dream, the man, and my attraction to him.

For about a year I dated many eligible men I met at both NASA Langley and the adjacent Langley Air Force Base. But after a year, I hadn't found anyone I liked in a special way. I didn't want just anybody. After all, I had turned down the millionaire. I wanted a soul mate, a twin soul, someone who was like the other half of my puzzle, a man whose destiny was intertwined with mine from the beginning of time.

I had read about twin souls and soul mates in books such as *Soul Mates* by Jess Stearn and *Twin Souls: Finding Your True Spiritual Partner* by Patricia Joudry and Maurice D. Pressman. A soul mate can be anyone with whom you have had a close personal relationship in a past life. We all have many soul mates. Often a soul mate relationship is full of conflict because the people come together to work out problems they each carry from previous lifetimes. I felt I'd had enough of that kind of relationship in my first marriage.

Whereas you can have many soul mates, only one of them is a twin soul or a twin flame, as Elizabeth Clare Prophet calls them in *Soul Mates and Twin Flames: The Spiritual Dimension of Love and Relationships*. A twin soul is a person whose connection with you is at a deep soul level. Some sources say that the twin soul is actually one soul split into a male and a female half. Other sources say the twin is a separate soul but has chosen to take the same path with your soul right from the beginning.

Whatever their origin, the basis of a twin soul relationship is supposed to be one of mutual helpfulness. Although there might be some smoothing of rough edges, karmically speaking, in a twin soul relationship, the two souls carry a feeling of having come home to each other. I wanted this kind of relationship, and so I prayed for a twin soul.

I'd heard about the 40-day prayer in which you thanked God for what you wanted as if you had it, in the name of Jesus the Christ. The prayer included the caution, "If it be Thy will," so that if you wanted something that might be harmful to you or others, God would protect you from yourself. Therefore, in my case, I prayed: "In the name of Jesus the Christ, thank You that I have found my twin soul, if it be Thy will."

You need to pray this prayer consistently for 40 days. If you miss even one day, you have to start all over again. The number 40 is supposedly a powerful Biblical number—Christ's 40 days in the wilderness, 40 days in the ark for Noah, etc.

I decided that since I hadn't yet found my twin soul the conventional way, I was going to try the 40-day prayer. Evidently nothing would happen until the last day or two—there was something powerful about consistently praying the same thing for 40 days.

Well, I began to pray. I did fine for about 20 days, and then I forgot a day so I had to start all over again. Unbelievably, on the

39th consecutive day of the prayer, I was in the cafeteria for some reason and literally ran right into Mr. Good Enough, the Man of my Dreams. I was in a hurry, running around a pillar, when I smashed into this immovable wall of chest. I screamed and jumped back. He grabbed my upper arms so I wouldn't fall and then released me gently. "Sorry," I mumbled at his chin, too afraid to look him in the face, my heart pounding in my ears. He smiled— that same soft quiet smile I'd seen in the dream. I ran.

Ever hopeful, I went back to eating in the cafeteria. I'd often see him looking at me. So that's what it took for him to notice me. I had to run into him! I'd smile over at him. He'd smile back—just like in high school. However, it never went further than a nod or a smile. Maybe he was as shy as I was. However, because of my prayer, I felt that, in spite of all the bashfulness in the world, I would have to eventually approach him.

This time it was an obligation to God. You don't ask for God's help, get it, and then throw it away. And anyway, God had already given me the dream about this man a year earlier. I had prayed "if it be Thy will," and if this was God's will, I had better do it!

I hadn't always been comfortable with the phrase "doing God's will."

In fact, for many years I had felt it was stupid and frightening. Who was this God, anyway, that I would do His will rather than what was best for me? From everything I'd known about God, especially the awful stories about Him in the Old Testament, He seemed to be a pretty heartless fellow.

However, over my years of spiritual searching, I had come to realize that God was personally mindful of me. I saw how the trials in my life, such as those devastating years in Phoenix, were actually learning experiences. Moreover, at a time when many families were floundering, my children and I had become inextricably closer because of our hardships.

So I had come to see that there was a greater knowingness guiding my life, an intelligence that had a larger picture than I did and that was deeply concerned with my survival and happiness. In fact, "God's will" began to mean something bigger than me, that knew more than I did, that cared for me profoundly, and could anticipate my needs better than I could.

Therefore, since it appeared that God intended that I get to know this man, I felt that I needed to carry out God's will to the best of my ability. I was also curious to see if the rest of the details in the dream were correct.

Finally one day when it seemed safe—there was hardly anyone in the cafeteria, and he was alone—I waited until he left the building, and then, as inconspicuously as possible, I walked quickly to catch up with him.

"Hi," I said.

He turned slowly, as in the dream, to face me.

I had never looked up-close at his face before. There was an amused look in his eyes as he glanced down at me. He had the most amazing sky-blue eyes.

"You thought I was someone else," he said as he made that soft smile I liked so much. His voice was a satiny baritone.

"No," I replied, "I dreamt about you." (Later he told me this was the best line he had ever heard.)

He invited me to his office. His name was John Chapman. We talked. I remember being so nervous that I sat sideways, only turning toward him with my face. He, on the other hand, sat comfortably, rocking slightly on his squeaky government-issue wooden swivel desk chair. He faced me squarely, his legs relaxed and apart, his hands on his thighs. After we talked awhile, he told me that I was one of the most interesting women he'd ever met.

After that, we occasionally had lunch together in the cafeteria. I found out that the details in the dream had been correct. He did have a "high up" house—built up on pilings because the house was so close to the coastal flood plain. Had he designed the house himself? Sort of. He found the design in a book and altered it to his liking. He wondered how I knew these things, since no one from work had ever visited him.

A Newfoundland honeymoon.

I also found out he had a black lab-type dog. I didn't need to ask about his friend because I'd already met him in the cafeteria. The man was swarthy, with dark hair, and his wife was dark-haired as well.

The satellite? Although John wasn't working with satellites when I first met him, he changed to Atmospheric Science after we were married. He now makes simulators for satellites.

One interesting aspect of our relationship is that when we were first dating, he told me that he kept having this feeling of déjà vu—as if he had met me before and already knew me. I had read that this was one of the signs of soul mates meeting. It gave me confirmation that he was feeling a sense of destiny with me as I was with him.

While dating, we also discovered that we had many things in common, especially our love of the outdoors—sailing and swimming. We often met at lunch hour for a swim.

When he asked me to marry him, about a year after I'd first approached him, he startled me by asking if I would feel the same way about him if I hadn't had the dream. It took me two days to think this over.

I thought about an incident at the ocean when I'd come close to drowning while caught in surf at a sandbar. John had rescued me. Financially, I was also drowning. My salary was just not enough to care for myself and the children. Although at first it rankled my pride, I had to admit I needed John's strength and stability. I also thought about all the fun I had now that he was in my life. Because of my heavy responsibilities raising the children by myself, I'd become so stern. He brought sunshine into my life. And I was madly in love with him. I said "Yes."

Don't get the idea that being married to the man of your dreams is like a fairy tale in which we live happily ever after. We are still human beings—imperfect by definition. During pre-marital counseling with our pastor, we learned how all of us choose a mate who will help us work out the unfinished business of our childhoods. Let's just say we fit each other's agendas. In addition, I believe we have had many lifetimes together and are still working out some hurts and misunderstandings.

However, this is like no other relationship I've ever had before.

For example, when we were first dating, John took my daughters and me to the State Fair. The main thing I wanted at the fair was that John would kiss me at the top of the ferris wheel, my favorite ride. However, I wouldn't even ask him to ride the ferris wheel with me because I didn't want to pressure him. When we reached the midway, John did not choose to go on the ferris wheel. So I stood in line by myself. Just as I was about to step on, John got on the gondola with me.

"You don't have to," I said.

"I don't care what ride I'm on as long as I'm with you," he replied.

Things were looking up, I thought. Maybe I'd even get that kiss at the top.

But, when the ride attendant put three surly pre-pubescent boys in the seat across from us, my heart sank. They looked like the type of kids who would carry sling-shots in a Mark Twain novel. John squeezed his 6'4" large-boned frame behind the safety bar and put his arm around me. I focused my gaze to the side of the boys because they had fixed their eyes on us.

As the aroma of caramel corn wafted around us, we started our ascent on the ferris wheel. Neon lights glowed below in the gathering dusk. From my vantage point high on the ferris wheel, I could see masses of little children, clutching balloons, tagging along beside their parents. Young women jostled their boyfriends who carried giant stuffed animals won at carnival games, and school-aged youngsters squealed and hooted on the rides below us.

I enjoyed the ferris wheel ride. It felt good sitting in the gondola with John's arm around me. I almost managed to ignore the surly-eyed youngsters sitting across from us. Too soon the ride came to an end.

As the attendant let passengers out of one gondola after another, the ferris wheel would stop for awhile and then move a space and stop again. We moved slowly until we were right at the top with a magnificent view of the fair. Now that the ferris wheel moved slowly, the rude young men especially focused their stares at us. Well, I thought, I'm never going to get a kiss with those brats staring at us.

Just then, John pulled me close and whispered, "Let's blow their minds." And he kissed me long and sweet.

So that's what it's like being married to the man of my dreams. Sometimes—not all the time—but every once in awhile, somehow, as if he can read my mind, he fulfills my dreams.

2

Trouble in Paradise

After we married, it appeared that I was about to live happily ever after with the man of my dreams. My three children were adjusting to their step-dad. My work was going well. Moreover, my new dream-man husband and I were madly and passionately in love.

But then I became pregnant. There was something wrong with the pregnancy. For a month I stayed home from work, keeping as still as possible in the hopes the baby within me would survive. But, at six weeks, it died, and I had to have a minor operation called a dilation and curettage (D & C).

After the operation, I started to gain weight rapidly.

I went to my family doctor and three obstetrician-gynecologists but none of them could help me. One doctor called it a hormonal imbalance and said it was not too uncommon after a late-in-life miscarriage.

I kept hoping my hormones would straighten themselves out because it was very important for me to look attractive for my dream man. John and I both had a tendency to put on the pounds. We ate healthy foods and had a regular exercise routine that included swimming, walking, and aerobics.

Following the miscarriage, however, I was gaining weight so rapidly that I had to buy a larger size of clothes every two or three weeks. After about four months of this with no help from the doctors, a friend suggested I see a hypnotherapist to tell my body I was no longer pregnant.

Normally I would have been wary of hypnotherapy. However, for a time I was gaining a pound a day. In four months, I'd gained over 50 pounds. I was just about ready to try anything.

I also knew that "America's greatest psychic," Edgar Cayce had given medical diagnoses while self-hypnotized. When he lost his speaking voice for a year and no doctors could help him, he had cured himself in trance. Maybe, while hypnotized, I could help myself as Cayce had done.

I had also read about past life regressions in which obese people had discovered that they were overweight in this lifetime because of dying of starvation in a previous incarnation. What if my life-long struggle with overweight had an origin in a past life?

Moreover, I was curious about my dream man. Had we known each other before? Was that why I knew him in the dream before I met him in real life?

For my hypnotherapist, I chose Lynn Sparrow, of Virginia Beach, who had been recommended by a friend. I felt safe with Lynn because she is a master hypnotist who teaches hypnotherapy and has years of affiliation with the Association of Research and Enlightenment (A.R.E.) as a speaker. Because the A.R.E. is the association built around the Edgar Cayce readings, I knew Lynn would be open to reincarnation. In addition, I wanted to work with a professional, rather than someone who dabbled in hypnosis, because I feared that I would be vulnerable while hypnotized.

I sat in a comfortable chair in Lynn's office. On the wall hung a beautiful painting of blue and green ocean waves. I love the sea. Looking at this painting made me feel that my association with Lynn would be positive.

I was also pleased that Lynn was pleasantly slender. I didn't want to work with a therapist, hypno- or otherwise, who had not solved their own weight problems. Although it was hard to believe because of her slender figure, Lynn told me she had a tendency to overweight but had used self-hypnosis to maintain a desirable weight. I wanted that cure.

We talked, partly so we could feel more comfortable together, and partly so we could be more focused on what we were about to do. I told Lynn that I was wary of hypnosis because for the last few years I had been praying, "Not my will but Thine, O Lord." I wanted to be sure that whatever I programmed into my unconscious would be directed by God. I was even willing to be fat forever if, for some reason presently inconceivable to me, it was God's will.

Lynn explained that God's will can be accessed in hypnosis through the superconscious where dwells the Christ Consciousness.

Upon hearing the word "Christ," I suddenly burst into tears. It brought to my remembrance an incident that had occurred about a year before my pregnancy. Prior to our marriage, John and I had gone for premarital counseling at his church. Although I loved to read the Bible, especially the parts about Jesus, I hardly ever went to church. Nonetheless, premarital counseling sounded like a good idea to me.

My future husband and I began to attend services. After one communion, as I knelt praying, I heard a voice say, "I died for you." I was filled and surrounded with an amazing Presence of Light, Love, and Forgiveness. It felt as if the Christ stood before me, His arms raised in blessing above me.

I started to cry, tears pouring through me and dripping on the pew. I tried to control my sobs, hoping that no one would notice me and that I was not embarrassing John, who knelt beside me.

Then I had the sense, from the Presence of the Christ before me, that my main sin was that I was too wishy-washy. As if in illustration, I saw the color beige in my mind.

That stopped the tears, because I hate that color. It does not look good on me because of my dark hair. It's the color for safe decorating, safe dressing—safety and caution in everything. I'd been fighting the concept of beige my whole life by wearing colorful clothes, being a photographer/writer, homeschooling, birthing at home and breast-feeding. But here I was, being confronted with my "beigeness," and I knew exactly what He meant.

I was afraid to really put myself on the line—to live a disciplined life, to stand up to people who operate through fear, even in the name of Christ. I was always afraid of being jeered at or ridiculed, of standing alone. And so I let things slide, seldom voicing a strong opinion of my own, not wanting to make a scene or court the disfavor of people who might have more power than I did. I was even afraid to stand up to an abusive or crazy person because I might be hurt or laughed at.

When I finished telling my story, I looked over at Lynn. Her eyes were open wide.

"So," she said, "there's more here than just your weight."

"I guess so," I answered.

"That's great," she said. She thought that likely my religious experience would figure in some way in the work we were about to undertake.

She asked if there was anything else that was important to consider before she actually started the hypnotizing process. I said that I really wanted to help women and children. At the time, I led meetings where I helped women who wanted to mother their babies by breastfeeding. In fact, I felt a special tenderness in my heart for all women who cared deeply for their babies and children.

Lynn said that likely my desire to help women and children would also figure in my hypnosis sessions. And so we began.

If you've never been hypnotized, you're probably wondering what it was like. Did Lynn use a pendulum, as we see in the movies? Did she say, "You are getting sleeeepy. Now, you are going deeper, deeeeper, deeeeeeper?" Well, she didn't, but she did modulate her voice so it sounded especially mellow and melodious as she emphasized certain words.

The first part of the hypnosis was concerned with relaxation. After asking me to sit as comfortably as possible, Lynn told me to close my eyes. Then, she made suggestions such as that my forehead and scalp were relaxed, my face, my eyes, my eyelids—various muscle groups from the top to the bottom of my body—were heavy.

I noticed that various muscles, especially in my arms and legs, twitched. Occasionally my eyes fluttered under my lids. When Lynn suggested I relax my mouth, my lips parted so that my mouth hung slightly open.

After awhile, Lynn made a suggestion to demonstrate to myself that I was really hypnotized. She told me to keep my eyes shut. Then she said, keeping in mind that my eyes were to remain shut, I should consciously try to open them. I tried, but I could not. No matter what I did, my eyelids stayed firmly in place.

Nonetheless, even though I knew my body was as relaxed as if it was asleep, my mind and senses were still very much awake. I would know when a car went by outside the office. I would hear the preprogrammed chime on my wristwatch announce the hour. Although I could not see her because my eyes were closed, I was aware that Lynn was watching me, I assumed, looking for physical signs that I was truly ready for the next part of the session. It helped that I liked Lynn and that she had come well-recommended. I felt safe with her.

Now that I was in a light trance, Lynn began making the suggestions we had previously discussed, such as that my body would resume its normal hormonal functioning, that I could see all my internal organs within me operating smoothly and efficiently and that I would enjoy drinking a lot of water to wash all the wastes out of my body.

When these suggestions were finished, Lynn brought me out of the hypnotic state. She did count as I've seen in the movies, from one to five: for example, "One, preparing to emerge; two, bringing with you everything you need both consciously and unconsciously; three, feeling a sense of peaceful rest and deep well-being within your body; four, feeling invigorated, rested, and alert; and five, able to open your eyes and come back feeling good."

Everything was taped, including beautiful music, which Lynn played on a separate tape machine from the one she used to tape the whole session. The tape of the hypnosis was mine. I could play it at home to reinforce the suggestions given. All of the dialogue during the hypnosis sessions in this book are taken from those tapes.

When I returned for my second hypnosis session with Lynn, I had gained almost seven pounds in a week.

Lynn said we would have to try another technique. She said that in dealing with persistent conditions like overweight, she often found it best to go back to the first incident causing the problem. It might be in this life or in one past. For example, a chubby child nicknamed "Oink" by vicious friends might grow up to be an adult with an unconscious belief that they were meant to be fat. If we could find the first experience that led to my struggle with overweight, we would find the best place to start to eradicate the problem.

Lynn told me of a very effective method for moving through time in which she would suggest that I float above a line or cord that represented time. In explaining the technique, she said she'd ask me to visualize time as a long line until I found the first time that dealt with my overweight. It would look like a spot down below me on the line. Then, Lynn said, she would suggest that I drift down into the line and begin to experience the incident.

It sounded good to me. I was ready. Lynn handed me a small clip-on microphone that I clamped onto the collar of my blouse. She began recording the session.

After making suggestions that thoroughly relaxed my body, Lynn brought me to the Light. I could see and feel this marvelously clear and bright Light, the same Light that I had encountered occasionally in my meditations. It surrounded me and was, at the same time, within me. Then Lynn acquainted me with the line that would take me to the place in my past where the tendency for being overweight had begun.

18

I could see this white line below me. I soared high above it like a great bird riding the air currents.

". . . and there are those questions that your eternal soul has brought," said Lynn, "those questions of life directions and wanting to be so sure that outcomes are aligned with your deepest, deepest soul's purpose, and God's will above all."

I was so relieved to hear that Lynn had remembered to include my desire to do God's will above all. I relaxed mentally as well as physically.

"And as you float so far above your line, as an eternal spiritual being, your unconscious mind, your deep, deep soul mind knows exactly where to take you . . . back to that time that will hold the answers about that physical balance, especially this issue of weight, the karmic causative factor that will cause you to share so much helpful insight with others . . ."

Then Lynn made the suggestion that I drift down into the line that represented time and notice what was around me.

"What are you aware of?" asked Lynn.

"The Light," I answered, softly.

The Light was so overpoweringly brilliant. It was everywhere. I could see it, feel it, smell it, taste it, hear it. It was around me and within me. It was pure white with a hint of gold, and it was blazing. It was so overwhelming that I could hardly speak.

Lynn said, "Sometimes it happens that the Light is a passageway to a very deep memory."

3

In the Beginning

When I listened to the tape of the hypnosis session afterwards, I could hear myself breathing deeply and swallowing. During the session I didn't want to say anything because I was embarrassed. I knew I was going to cry.

The feelings in a past life regression are amazingly intense. And although I could neither see nor hear anything, I was becoming aware that I was feeling totally and devastatingly lonely.

"I have feelings of being lonely," I said in a choking voice, and I started to cry. I could see nothing but just felt lonely to the depths of my being.

Lynn sounded so kind. "Yes. Just let those feelings lead you into what you need to know. You may find, in fact, that those lonely feelings will soon open up into a scene."

I continued to cry softly, breathing deeply. Finally I began to see where I was. "Well, there's a sense of . . . a cave . . . and . . . it's dark. And . . . there's . . . stars?" I was having trouble finding words to describe what I was experiencing.

Lynn asked, "Are you male or female? Are you a child or an adult?"
"I'm a woman. I'm an adult. I'm naked." I hesitated. 'I'm gorgeous!' I said, delighted with how beautiful I looked—so

different from the shame and disappointment I usually felt about my body.

Lynn's voice rose with interest as if we had just hit a bull's eye. "I see!"

I struggled with words to describe what I was experiencing, "I'm wild. I mean . . . I belong to the Earth. I'm good . . . I'm uncorrupt—that's it."

"Do you live alone?" asked Lynn.

"So far," I said. I didn't seem to have a sense of time. All I knew was that I was alone. "And there's this sense, maybe . . . of listening."

"Yes, that's a good idea," said Lynn. "Why don't you listen for awhile."

I stayed very quiet in the cave, looking out the entrance and listening. It felt like that kind of listening when you strain so hard to hear something that you can almost hear your ears buzzing. "I'm alert and I'm waiting."

"Who are you waiting for?" asked Lynn.

"Well, I think it's John. I guess he's been hunting." Now I knew that I had known John in a past life. However, I was having trouble with my feelings in the past life regression. In this life, John is my beloved. However, the impression I had from this past life was that I was not looking forward to his return. He also seemed to be some kind of a beast or monster. Therefore, I was not listening with anticipation but with a mixture of dread and disgust.

"It's somehow different." There was something else that my conscious mind could not decipher. Not only was John different, but also I was becoming aware that in some very significant way, I was different.

"It doesn't seem as if I'm as solid as I am [now]. It's different." I tried to understand who and what I was. "I'm . . . translucent or something."

I appeared to be floating. I wasn't solid. My mind searched and searched to understand. I neither felt nor looked like any person or thing I now know or have ever known. I tried to find the words to describe it. And then the realization came.

"It's about being stuck!" I cried. I began to wail, calling out in pain and sorrow. "I'm so sad!" I sobbed.

"Just let it go," soothed Lynn.

"It's like being amber somehow and being stuck in the cave. I can sort of glide, but I can't get free." I was like an amber-colored genie who slid out of a lamp, with a swirl of smoke extending from my waist down to the ground. There were no legs, just a translucent half-body which was amber-colored. My torso looked like a beautiful naked adult dark-haired female that floated above the floor of the cave. The torso was see-through, as was the "smoke" that extended from the waist down to the ground. I hovered to the right of something that looked like a burnt-out fire on the floor of the cave. I strained toward the mouth of the shelter.

"If you can get free, where would you go?" asked Lynn.

"There's a light place that will take me away home," I sobbed. And then I began to wail again. "I want to go home." Then quieter and with determination, "I really want to go home."

"Tell me about your home. You say it's a light place," said Lynn.

Lynn hadn't understood me. There was a light place that would take me home. Across the valley from the cave, on the crest of a hill, there was something that looked like a flying saucer. It was lit up and oval shaped. But I knew it only looked like a flying saucer. It was actually a vortex of swirling clouds, lighted in the night. It operated like a gate. It would take me to another world, my home.

I was not yet ready to say the name of my home because it was too shocking for my conscious mind. But I had heard and seen the word "Arcturus." My home was an entirely different star system! I was an alien!

Eek!!!

There are all kinds of people who believe that aliens presently visit the Earth. I am not one of them. It's not that I can't entertain the notion. It's just that the idea is simply too strange for me, and I have not had a personal experience. I can say, "Yes, it's possible," because all kinds of things are possible. And although I love such science fiction entertainments as *Star Wars, Star Trek, E.T: The Extraterrestrial*, etc., I see them more as extensions of our present-day space program—preparing our civilization for space travel.

Furthermore, I know that authors such as Ruth Montgomery, Whitley Strieber, and Harvard psychiatrist Dr. John Mack are convinced that space aliens walk the Earth.

I try to keep an open mind. I am open to the possibility that beings from other planets in other star systems could visit the Earth. After all, we have a space program that hopes to visit other star systems some day.

But me, an alien? Outrageous! Look at me. I am a human being—brown hair, green eyes, five-foot-three, chubby, pinkish-beige skin. If I was an alien from Arcturus (according to a June 1999 *Fate* magazine article by Dawn Baumann Brunke), I should be three or four feet tall and have green skin.

On the other hand, many people are convinced that aliens visit the Earth today and are sure the United States government has kept secret the 1947 crash of an alien spaceship at Roswell, New Mexico. In Philip J. Corso's *The Day After Roswell*, the retired army colonel affirms that much of our modern technology was developed from the wreckage of the Roswell crash. If aliens have been visiting the Earth throughout all time, it is conceivable that some have become trapped here.

In his book *Past Lives, Future Loves*, Dick Sutphen, who hypnotically regresses roomfuls of people at a time, says that when he asks people to go to their first life on Earth, six to seven percent report that they were first a being from another world. Perhaps numbers of us originally came from other star systems.

A beautifully-written book, *Songs of the Arcturians: The Arcturian Star Chronicles*, by Patricia L. Pereira helped me to feel more comfortable with the idea of visitors from Arcturus coming to Earth.

In the Beginning

As for Arcturus, it is a yellow-orange star in the constellation Bootes, 37 light years away from us. Although 37 light years sounds like a long way off, it is actually a relatively close star.

The June 1999 *Fate* article, mentioned earlier, catalogues different types of extraterrestrials. According to Brunke, Arcturians may be "guardians of higher consciousness" and may "represent a prototype of humanity's future." They can evidently move objects with their minds and communicate telepathically, educating humanity and defending us against hostile extraterrestrials. I was glad to see that. Just in case I really was an alien, at least Arcturians appeared to be a pretty decent lot.

Under hypnosis I had said that there was a Star Gate which was used as a doorway between star systems. I was distressed because I could no longer go through it. On the other side of the Star Gate, I would no longer be restricted by earth time and space. I would be on star-time.

The Star Gate functioned similarly to the transporter in the popular science-fiction TV series Star Trek, as in "Beam me up, Scotty," or perhaps, in this case, "Beam me out!" The only way you could go through was in a non-physical form.

As long as I was "stuck" in the physical, I could not pass through the Star Gate to my home. However, this physical body in which I found myself was not even solid. It was a wisp-of-smoke, a thought form. Nonetheless, it had enough of a connection with the Earth that I could not free myself from the planet.

Eventually I did say out loud that Arcturus was my home. "It's real special somehow, and I'm lonely." I began to cry again. Almost as an afterthought I added, "I'm ashamed, too."

Lynn's voice changed as if we'd hit another bull's eye, "You're ashamed. What are you ashamed of?"

"I'm ashamed of getting stuck."

"What was your original intention in coming here?"

"Exploration."

Lynn decided we should discover how I came to be stuck. She made the suggestion that I go back to the time when I could move easily to the place that was lit up on the hill and get home.

To my surprise, I found myself to be a light beam. I looked similar to a line of glowing Morse code—a vertical line of three different-length parts.

As a light beam, I played and danced on undulating waves of color, especially pink, blue, mauve, and purple, which extended as far as I could see. As the waves of colors moved, I heard sounds, like music, that coincided with the various colors and their movement in relationship with each other. The music was beautiful and constant, but changing, like a sea of voices. I could feel the music within me. Everything was experienced—the colors, the waves and the music—as vibrations.

"And what are you aware of as a light beam?" asked Lynn.

"I really like the sense of vibrations in me and through me. They feel really good. And I sort of dance on it all." I was happy and carefree and danced with joy on the waves of vibrations.

Lynn asked me if I had a companion.

I sighed as if I yearned for a friend and answered, "Not yet."

"What happens next?" asked Lynn.

"Well, I experiment and go deeper, and it's murkier. That's OK." Why did I have to say, "That's OK."? Were my actions somehow becoming questionable?

I continued, "It feels unusual. It's like a pipe organ—where it makes those deep, deep sounds. I go down into that sound. I really like it. And I want to experience it. It makes me vibrate."

I was getting deeper and deeper into the vibrations. No longer merely dancing on them, I was now *in* them, feeling the vibrations wafting over and through me. "My light isn't as bright," I said. The deeper I went, the darker and murkier the colors became, and the deeper the vibrations resonated that accompanied them.

In the Beginning

Lynn asked, "Is there anyone with you?"

I paused and then answered with sadness in my voice, "No, he's down below."

"Who is he?"

I sighed. "It's John," I answered, starting to cry in distress. "Why I had to go down there, I don't know. I just got attracted to it."

It?

I now experienced the Earth as a murky, orange-brown haze without undulating waves or color, accompanied by the deepest bone-rattling tones similar to the growl of a great pipe organ. Despite the strangeness of this alien (for me) landscape, I was reveling in the deep, deep vibrations. It was new and exciting.

Deep in the static gloom that vibrated so gravely, I was beginning to see the shape of a creature that looked like a bear or an ape. He stood by something that looked like the trunk of a tree.

"I want to play with him," I said and then hesitated. "And so, I do." I sounded embarrassed.

"Do you enjoy this?" asked Lynn. "What kind of play do you have?"

"Well, it's sexual." I hesitated. "The word is 'sex'. It's got to be . . . because he's an ape or something . . . an animal."

Deep in the orange-brown shadows of the Earth, I found myself to be a small cloud that caressed over and under and around this black form in the shape of a bear or ape almost on all fours. I flitted around him, enjoying the deep feelings vibrating through me. I moved like a wind over his back, between his legs, and along his arms and buttocks. I could feel a corresponding tremor from the beast. It was exciting, something I had never experienced before. "And I find it very interesting," I said, trying to sound as nonchalant as possible.

"And then what happens?" asked Lynn.

I sighed, "Then comes . . . being in the cave."

When Lynn and I talked after I was out of trance, we agreed that that this session seemed to be about my first lifetime on Earth.

The shame was a clue to the reason for my being overweight. It seemed I was not only ashamed of my body, but I was also ashamed that I had a body at all. I felt that the body was keeping me from returning "home."

For weeks after this session, the intense yearning for home accompanied me wherever I went and whatever I did. The longing was so strong, it felt like I could taste it, as if each nerve in my body vibrated with yearning and as if each cell cried out, "Home!"

As long as I had a body, I could not go "home" through the Star Gate—even if that body was just a wisp-of-smoke. The overweight was a constant reminder that I was solid rather than my real self which was pure light.

This "first causative factor" was such a surprise. Lynn said she had never encountered a first lifetime before in her work.

4

Fat Karma

During the time of my hypnotherapy, my middle child, Clair, was attending Old Dominion University in Norfolk, Virginia. Since the university was on my way home, I stopped by to see her. We sat in an empty sixth-floor study room in Clair's dormitory. She didn't have any classes until later in the day.

"So what did you find out in your hypnosis session?" she asked.

"Would you believe I'm an alien?"

"Yeah, sure, Mom."

"No, really. I'm supposed to be from Arcturus."

Clair looked at me through lowered lids. "Well, if you're an alien, then we all are."

"That just might be it," I replied.

From the table in the middle of the room, I looked out the window to the street below. Trees were changing color. A scattering of gold, red, and brown leaves decorated the pavement.

"Anything else?" she asked.

I knew Clair would enjoy hearing the next part, "You were once my older sister." After the first life regression, Lynn had led me to other lifetimes contributing to my overweight.

Clair's eyebrows lifted. "Cool," she said.

"I loved you with all my heart," I said. You were devoted to me—taking care of me and teaching me things."

"What were we doing?" she asked.

"We seemed to be somewhere like Africa. There were bulrushes, and we were fishing in a dugout canoe at night. The moon was shining. Fish would come up to the surface to eat stuff floating on the water. We held string that dangled a hook made of bone just under the water, and when we'd see a fish in the moonlight, we'd jerk the hook under its jaw."

"We were Black?" Clair's blue eyes widened. Her pink mouth dropped open. A wisp of blonde hair fell over her forehead

"We were so black," I said, "that at night, all you could see of us were our teeth and the whites of our eyes."

"Wow."

I remembered our round thatched houses and how I pounded grain in a hollowed-out log with a long stick in the company of the other women of the tribe. John, who was chief of the tribe, was my husband again. I remembered how he had sat with me when I was dying. "I got to see my death," I told Clair.

"You saw yourself die?" exclaimed Clair.

"I relived it."

"Was it awful?"

"Not at all. I was an old woman—my hair, stiff and gray. It was nighttime, stars shone above me. I was laid out on some kind of bier. My breathing was raspy and slow. Standing around me in a semi-circle were all the people, young and old, in our tribe, helping me with the transition. It was our custom to say farewell in this manner."

My heart filled with the memory of so many people who loved me. John, a tall muscular older man with blue-black skin, sat on the bier beside me holding my hand in the darkness.

I looked up at Clair.

"You had died before me . . . and when I made the transition, there you were waiting for me."

"I was? How did I look?"

"That's strange." I searched my mind to remember anything. "As far as I can recall, I saw nothingness, a void. I didn't see anything. But I knew it was you."

"It sounds as if I'm 'me' whether I'm an African lady who's your older sister, an American girl who's your daughter, or some kind of presence in the afterlife."

"I guess so," I said. We looked at each other. I smiled, thinking how special Clair was to me. She reached across the table and gave me a big hug.

"So did you find out why you're overweight?" Clair asked.

I told her the story about getting caught in the physical and how my overweight was a constant reminder so I would strive to free myself. Then I remembered how the African lifetime had reinforced the obesity. "You know, in Africa, I was slender and nymph-like—just how I'd like to be now. But I'd been captured by John's tribe when I was a child. They were tall and big-boned. I spent my life wishing to be big like them."

Clair sucked in her breath. "You got your wish. You are big. Except you aren't tall; you're wide."

"Sad but true," I replied.

"It makes you want to be careful what you wish for," she said.

"Exactly. Maybe if I keep wishing to be slender in this life, I'll end up starving in my next. Isn't it the Buddhists who believe we have to live without desire?"

On the drive home, I thought about another lifetime having to do with obesity that Lynn and I had explored. In France I had made fun of overweight people. Vain and self-centered, I was part of the aristocracy just before the French Revolution. In the hypnosis session, I found myself in an ornate horse-drawn coach on the way to meet my betrothed. It was an arranged marriage based on the linking of our two families' land holdings. I had never met the young man before. When I arrived at my future husband's estate, I didn't know which of the men was my betrothed because his advisors were standing with him. However, when I realized it was the fat young man, I laughed in his face. Thereafter, I ridiculed him and any other overweight person I encountered throughout that lifetime. In this life, I'm finding out how terrible they felt to be ridiculed. Our whole society ridicules fat people.

The Cayce past-life readings show many instances where mockery in one lifetime creates the same problem in a future life—but in the person doing the ridiculing. In one reading, a young woman, who had been an athlete in the games that have become our modern-day Olympics, had sneered at people who were overweight. She had come to Cayce in the present because of obesity. I have always thought it ironic that overweight people are mercilessly critical of people with weight problems, themselves included. Could it be that their heartless attitude continues from the past life that created their obesity?

Interestingly, one of the most important factors contributing to obesity, discovered by University of California innovator Laurel Mellin, author of *The Solution: Six Winning Ways to Weight Loss*, is what she calls, "weightism . . . discrimination based on body weight." She has found that, among many other factors, very often people cannot permanently let go of weight until they can love their bodies while they are fat. Although Mellin does not mention reincarnation in her book, I thought that this cure, called "Body Pride," reverses the mocking attitude that created the obesity in a past life.

Gina Cerminara, author of *Many Mansions*, Edgar Cayce's story of reincarnation, devotes an entire chapter to the karma of mockery, not only having to do with obesity but also related to many other physical ailments and difficult life circumstances, such as homosexuality. The karma of mockery certainly makes a person want to love other fellow humans—to be tolerant rather than prejudiced.

Before I went for hypnotherapy, I had wondered if I might have starved to death in a past life. In books on reincarnation, by Dick Sutphen, I had read that often a lifetime of hunger resulted in

Fat Karma

a present life filled with an unquenchable hunger. I discovered that I had been excruciatingly hungry in the dungeon where I was imprisoned before I was guillotined to death during the French Revolution. My constant current feelings of hunger and the fear that I won't get enough food, as irrational as they are in this land of plenty, have followed me into this lifetime. In addition, during the past life memory of this time in the French Revolution, as I stood in the wobbly cart that took me to the guillotine, I remarked to Lynn that luckily my skirt was made of heavy, thickly gathered material so it hid the stark bones of my hips. In this present lifetime, I carry most of my weight on my hips.

I also saw the reason for other physical ailments in this lifetime. While in the dungeon, I was tortured with red-hot pokers which were shoved up my anus. In this life I suffer with hemorrhoids. Chronic tonsillitis and a thyroid condition in this lifetime were due to the beheading.

This is not to say that everyone who has a weight problem in this lifetime desired to be big, was starved in a dungeon, and/or mocked fat people in past lives. Or that hemorrhoids necessarily result from torture with red hot pokers, or thyroid problems come from a beheading. However, these are certainly possibilities.

As the French Revolution hypnosis session drew to a close, I experienced a healing. After reliving my death, which was quick and painless, Lynn brought me back to the Light and made the suggestion that I allow angelic beings to heal my body of the effects of the torture and beheading.

The angelic beings had curly hair, bright shining eyes and pretty bow-shaped mouths. They were small and cherubic, fluttering on wings that blurred as their chubby little bodies flitted over me, healing my throat of the beheading and my tailbone which had been bent too far to the right by the metal poker.

Because the angelic beings worked on my non-physical body, the healing changes would not occur immediately but would take a while to percolate into the flesh. Nonetheless, at the end of the healing I heard that "There'll be other adjustments I will make myself." I wondered what that meant.

33

Within a week, I found out. I fell down the stairs and severed the tendon that held my left ankle to my heel. The x-rays showed a bone chip, which should have been attached to my heel, floating at the end of the severed tendon. Had my tailbone also been adjusted when I tumbled down the stairs? Were these the "other adjustments" that had been foretold in the previous session?

It was around this time that I began to suspect something unusual had been set in motion, starting with my dream about the man I would marry. Therefore, although my ankle, in its splint, throbbed painfully as I hobbled on crutches, I was determined to attend my next appointment, which was scheduled for November 17, 1995. Something was happening to me, and I needed to know what. Although I couldn't drive, Clair, who was home for the Thanksgiving holiday, kindly agreed to drive me to Lynn's office.

At the end of this session, which had been set aside to explore my lifetime in Atlantis, I had a vision.

5

The Vision

As Lynn started to summarize the Atlantean lifetime, she asked, "What is the reason for your needing to reconnect with this old, old memory now, in terms of the unfolding path that you're following in your life?"

I answered, "My sense is to gather the faithful . . . It's that there are people that could be trusted . . . that are good."

I saw young people bowed on one knee. They were frightened and in despair because our world seemed insane to them. Around them swirled a maelstrom of darkness. The evil and selfishness around them fell away as they began to arise and glow. They were the Golden Ones, the hope of the world. Their souls were aligned with God—to bring in a New World in which there would be a thousand years of peace. It was my purpose to awaken them to their destiny.

They were reincarnating at this time to help humanity through the transition that was imminent. During the time that Atlantis was breaking up, they had taken on this task of bringing in a New World by choosing to reincarnate in the present time.

I was to write a book explaining the true history of the soul on Earth to provide them and humanity with a better understanding of life in preparation for this New World.

I saw a fountain. It was both golden and turquoise. "It's Aquarius!" I said, and then I understood that the young people were the harbingers of the Age of Aquarius, of which we have heard so much that it has almost become banal. Nonetheless, although "New Age" and "Age of Aquarius" have become so commonplace as to be advertising slogans, they are phrases that actually have great significance for our times.

However, I did not see the Aquarius astrological symbol as it is usually depicted: two wavy lines, portraying water, because Aquarius is the sign of the water-bearer. Instead, I saw water gushing upward like a fountain out of what appeared to be a golden pyramid. It was a lovely symbol, and I liked it much better than the double-wavy lines as an emblem of an age which is supposed to be characterized by harmony and peace.

I saw the young people rise from their knees and begin to glow. They turned to the right to a place that floated and that seemed to have the three Great Pyramids on it.

And then I said something that I am still, as I write this, trying to accept:

"This is the next race being born."

What was that about? The next race being born? I had a distant recollection of reading or hearing something about root races from the 19th century mystic, Madame Blavatsky. I was also vaguely aware that there was something in the Cayce readings on a Fifth Root Race soon to be born. Was the Fifth Root Race the new race referred to in my vision? If it was, why was I involved in it?

My conscious mind began to panic at the thought of writing a book about something so unusual. "I have fears about results— whether I'll be successful or whether people will laugh at me," I said to Lynn while hypnotized.

I felt totally inadequate to the task. It was one thing to be curious about reincarnation and to have dreamt about the man I would marry. But to write or speak about something as strange as a new type of being? I couldn't do that. People would label me a flake, John might leave me, my children could lose respect for me. What would my parents think?

As my fears mounted, I realized that there was someone standing beside me. "Have no fear, I am with you," I heard. It was the same voice I had heard in church. I saw sandaled feet and the bottom of a white robe.

The tears welled up in me. "I'm such a little person," I said, sniffling, then understood that everything was inconsequential if I had His help beside me. "I have help right on my right shoulder."

Suddenly I saw myself as a flower. Instead of being a human being sitting in the recliner in Lynn's office, I was a white lotus. "It unfolds, and it has golden stamens that reach up," I said.

The main thing I know about the lotus is that the Buddha is typically depicted sitting on a lotus. It is also associated with the water lily, a plant that rises out of murky waters to produce a beautiful flower.

Amazingly, the image of myself as a lotus was very comforting. It was as if it said that I could rise out of my own murk to produce something beautiful.

I heard from my helper on my right, "Just do it. The results are with Me. Let go. . . . Let go."

6

The Golden Ones

After the session, Clair tucked me, my swollen foot, and the crutches into the car.

As we drove to a restaurant, I turned to Clair and said, "You know what? I just remembered that when I was a bit older than you, I ripped the tendon in my left ankle at the end of my bicycle trip."

Clair knew about my solo adventure at the age of 22 when I'd traveled in the Canadian Maritimes on a bicycle. I continued as she drove, "It took over six months before I could walk normally again." I blew out as I remembered how painful it had been to walk. Nonetheless, when I was younger, I had managed without crutches. Now I could barely manage with crutches. "I'm just wondering how long it's going take to heal this time."

After we got settled at the restaurant and put in our order, Clair asked, "Well, what happened this time?"

I wasn't exactly sure where to begin. On the one hand, it was so outrageous I didn't know if it was even worth mentioning. On the other hand, in the midst of all kinds of predictions of doom by both psychics and conventional scientists—Armageddon, ozone holes, greenhouse gases, and overpopulation—I had seen that on the other side of our problems, there was a beautiful world ahead.

Was it worth saying something on the chance that there might be some truth to it?

Finally I decided that it might be helpful, so I told Clair about the vision. "There really is hope," I said.

"Mom," she said, "you wouldn't believe the number of people who are truly lost at the dorm—doing drugs until they're wasted, getting drop-dead drunk, and having indiscriminate sex. There are so many people full of despair."

"This is for your generation," I said.

"It's like numbers of young people all over the world have this memory deep within them. I called them the Golden Ones. I'm supposed to write a book to *awaken* them, whatever that means."

"Well, maybe, just like you didn't know you had this information in you," she said, "they may have similar memories buried in their unconscious minds as well."

"Makes sense," I replied. "In their unconscious minds they may know to expect these changes. Of course, they don't know it yet. I guess that's what I'm supposed to do—awaken them."

"Cool," she said.

"You are the ones who will bring in the next generation," I said, "According to what I saw, it seems as if there's supposed to be a new race being born."

Clair put her hands on the table and leaned back. "What?" she said.

I leaned forward and spoke softly. "I'm not sure what it means. I said that this would be the birth of a new race."

Clair leaned toward me, "You aren't making sense," she said slowly.

I cleared my throat and whispered, "I think it's supposed to be about a new type of being—a root race—not race by skin color. You know, a root race. I think I read about it somewhere . . ."

"What exactly do you mean?" she asked, sitting up straight and fixing me with an intense stare that has been one of her characteristics since babyhood.

"Well, as far as I can tell, it's like we've been in different life forms."

She was still staring at me quizzically. I wracked my brain for something that resonated with Clair's own personal viewpoint. I knew she was interested in Native American philosophy.

"OK, you know the Hopi Indians? We drove through their reservation when we lived in Arizona and went camping in Colorado—remember, the four corners area . . .?"

"Yeah, we had our pictures taken there . . ."

"Well, they have a tradition that there's been something like four worlds before the present one and each was destroyed by giant earth upheavals. It's like in each of those different worlds we were different kinds of beings—the root races."

Clair leaned back with a look of concentration on her face, "Yeah, OK, I get it."

"We're supposed to be on the brink of the fifth."

"OK . . ." She blinked a number of times as she assimilated what I was saying.

I continued, "These young people that I'm supposed to awaken either are this Fifth Root Race, or else they're going to birth them." I looked at her face to see if she was shocked by what I was saying. "In any case, it's pretty wild—pretty strange."

She shrugged. "Sounds pretty cool to me. Maybe I'm one of them."

"Yeah." I smiled, wondering what kind of being this Fifth Root Race would be like and if it meant that my grandchildren would look really strange.

"Anything else?" asked Clair.

I was surprised that Clair was taking this information, which to me was so outrageous, so nonchalantly. I found myself relaxing. "Oh," I said suddenly, remembering something else. "There's this whole thing about the Great Pyramid—you know how I've been crazy about it my whole life."

Clair knew about my fascination with ancient Egypt and the Great Pyramid.

"You won't believe this!" I said.

Clair gave me "the stare" as if to say, "Try me."

"Supposedly the Great Pyramid has something to do with it."

Clair looked at me intently, an inquisitive look on her face.

"Sounds pretty flaky, don't you think?" I said.

"I think it's interesting," she said.

"Yeah, but you're my daughter," I said. "You've been raised to be open-minded. There's all kinds of people who are absolutely terrified of anything unusual,"

"Who cares about them?" said Clair. "That's their hang-up."

"Clair," I said in a whisper, leaning so far forward that I was almost lying on the table. "*I* think it's flaky."

"Oh," said Clair as she flashed a quick smile. "You're up-tight about writing about it."

"You're telling me!" I said. "I'm even afraid the waitress will overhear us." I looked around to see if the waitress was approaching with our meal.

Clair leaned forward over the table to look at me face to face and said in a conspiratorial tone, "Mom, nobody in this restaurant cares if it's your mission to awaken the Golden Ones who are going to bring in the Fifth Root Race. If anything, they think we're discussing a science fiction movie."

I sat up, tried to smile and adjusted the scarf at my neck as the waitress arrived and placed our meals in front of us. I recalled the sin of being wishy-washy from my church experience. After the waitress left, I said, "Do you really think so?"

Clair's face softened. "Don't worry about it," she said. "Just write it straight. Tell how it happened. That's all you have to do. Those who need to hear it will get it."

"You're not going to leave me because everyone else thinks I'm nuts?" I asked.

"You're not nuts, Mom," replied Clair. "You're strange, unusual, a pain in the butt sometimes, but you're definitely not nuts. Don't worry about it."

"Thanks." I grinned at her backwards assurance.

"Just think," said Clair, "how many people are fascinated with the Great Pyramid. You're not the only one. They've probably got memories buried in their unconscious minds just like you. Maybe they helped build it or took part in whatever happened there so long ago."

I thought for a minute as I chewed on my salad. "You know, that makes a lot of sense. Carl Jung said that for him one of the proofs that Christ had actually lived and overcome death was that the Christ-based religions spread so easily throughout the world. To him that meant that the resurrection must be an archetypal thought form buried in the unconscious of people throughout the world. In the same way, why not an archetype about the Great Pyramid? There are many mysterious ruins throughout the world, but there isn't another pile of rock that fires people's imaginations like the Great Pyramid. Napoleon was there, and Isaac Newton used its measurements to prove his theory of gravity."

Clair was smiling widely.

"OK, I get it," I said. "The reason why this might not be so outrageous to a lot of people is because I'm not the only one who has memories about the purpose of the Pyramid. And there's also the Golden Ones—the ones ready to be awakened. They've got to have the subconscious information in them because in the vision they were all drawn to it."

Clair was beaming.

It turned out that my son and youngest daughter were also supportive and found the information intriguing. On the other hand, John, with his scientific mind, thought that I had an amazing imagination. He enjoyed the stories I told of my hypnosis sessions, but he never took either me or the stories seriously.

*   *   *

Since the publication of *The Golden Ones*, I have been doing book singings and giving seminars in the United States and Canada. One question that many people ask me is, "Are the Golden Ones the same as the Indigo Children?"

The Indigo Children: The New Kids Have Arrived by Lee Carroll and Jan Tober, came out in 1999. The book says that many

43

children being born recently have a new aura, which is indigo. These children have an innate technological expertise, carry a feeling of entitlement, are often characterized as antisocial by schools, are difficult to discipline by authoritarian methods, know what they need, and often see better and more creative solutions to established methods. They can also have a low tolerance for frustration and can become violent if they are not handled well. Indigos may be diagnosed as having Attention Deficit Disorder (ADD) because of their unruly nature. The authors suggest that many of these children have been incorrectly diagnosed.

Other people asked about the Crystal Children. In *The Crystal Children: A Guide to the Newest Generation of Psychic and Sensitive Children*, Doreen Virtue describes this group of children, many of whom have been born since about 1996. Unlike the Indigos, these children do not have an angry edge to them. They are much more docile and may be incorrectly diagnosed as autistic since many of them do not begin to talk until later than is considered normal. The Crystals also are very sensitive to discordant environments, feel comfortable with nature, are psychic, often remember their past lives, have a talent for healing, and may profess profound insights at an early age.

In *Edgar Cayce on the Indigo Children*, co-authors Peggy Rose Day and Susan Gale describe another category of child, the Psychic Child. They explain that Edgar Cayce predicted that groups of remarkable children would begin to incarnate at the end of the twentieth century. The authors show how these children are appearing throughout the world.

James Twyman also describes psychically gifted Bulgarian children who possess spiritual knowledge beyond their years in *Emissary of Love: The Psychic Children Speak to the World*. They ask the people of the world to act as if we are all emissaries of love.

So, which ones are the Golden Ones? Are they the Indigos, the Crystal, the Psychics, or the Emissaries?

Actually, they could be any one of these children. The Golden Ones are children, some of whom may be adults now, who came here to be of help. They are not violent. They are loving. They lived through the destructions and conflicts in Atlantis. Their souls knew to expect a time in the future—our time—when we would again be technologically advanced and teetering on self-annihilation. At the soul level they have dedicated themselves to being of help during this very difficult time.

They have an affinity with nature. Although they are saddened by wanton destruction of the natural world and cruelty between peoples, their response is to find a way to do something about it. They are less likely to rebel and more likely to look for a solution. They are more likely to find groups that are making improvements in the world than they are likely to align themselves with groups that self-centeredly cause trouble to vent frustration.

The Golden Ones, although they are motivated at a soul level by memories of the mistakes made in Atlantis, may or may not consciously remember their experiences during that long time ago. They are also likely psychic, intuitive, and creative. Because of the knowledge and ideals they carry, they may be wiser than their years.

Therefore, I concluded that the Golden Ones could be interspersed among any of the categories of children I had read about. They were not synonymous with any one type. In fact, they were not a type at all, because the Golden Ones referred more to their soul purpose than to the way they appeared in the physical.

However, in researching the above books and talking to people about the Indigos, Crystals, Psychic, and Emissaries, I began to wonder if I had simply made up the Golden Ones. No one else seemed to be talking about them.

And then, in late 2003, I received an email from a Honolulu reader of *The Golden Ones*. She thanked me for the book because it helped her to better understand the Golden Ones. She had first heard about them from someone else.

Yay! I was not the only one talking about the Golden Ones. It turned out that Dr. Devra West, of the Sacred Arts Institute, a spiritual healing school in Montana, had been channeling Master Maitreya, and had been receiving information about the Golden Ones.

To my delight, her information paralleled mine. She also said that the Golden Ones would help to bring in the thousand years of peace. In her Teachings of Wisdom, The Unity Transmissions, she entreats her followers to withdraw their negative thought forms.

I realized that my sunrise exercises, described in the next two chapters, Chapter Seven, God is Greater, and Chapter Eight, The Light Without, resembled her teaching to eliminate negative thought forms. Whereas she suggested a nightly two-hour session that retrained thought, my guides had shown me a way of changing thought by turning around the negativity we carried in the cells of our body with the sunrise exercises. They showed me a simple way of teaching ourselves, at the cell level, that light overcomes darkness.

Dr. Devra West also said that by turning our thoughts to the positive instead of the negative, more of the Golden Ones would be born, something which I had not said but which delighted me. She also described the Golden Ones as being spiritually awakened at birth so that by the age of seven they could be enlightened teachers, again something I had not received from my guides, but something that also made me feel happy to know.

I'm also happy to have received emails from people who have dreamt they or their children are one of the Golden Ones. Sometimes, they are people who haven't even read my book. That means that they didn't dream about the Golden Ones as a result of a suggestion from my book or from Dr. Devra West's channeling.

Sometimes these people have contacted me via email after doing an internet search to better understand their dreams. They are connecting with the information through their own subconscious minds.

Most gratifying for me are the parents and grandparents who come to me with stories of their children and grandchildren who are so gifted psychically or even just amazingly wise. If you remember, Dr. Devra West of the Sacred Arts Institute says that the Golden Ones will know the Sacred Teachings by age seven.

Many of these young people also have memories of Atlantis. For example, one young woman remembers leading people to safety lands when Atlantis was breaking up. In the end, she perished during that Atlantean experience while trying to help so many. In this lifetime she is highly motivated to be of help to people when disasters strike.

Many of these young people do not have memories but they are sincerely and dedicatedly involved in bettering our world. They may feel discouraged by the forces that work against them, but I hope that the information here and in other places, will encourage them to keep hopeful.

7

God Is Greater

I wondered what I should write or say to the Golden Ones, the young people who are bringing in the Fifth Root Race and the Age of Aquarius. In my next session I would find out.

I was told that this was a message for everyone: we live our lives as if we are greater than God. This is the basis of our undoing.

Next I expected to hear a diatribe on church attendance or our inhumanity to our fellow man, but instead I saw people throughout the world in primitive societies raising their arms in greeting to the rising sun.

Then I heard a diatribe on our need to interact with the natural world. "It seems like it takes so much time to bother to be in sunlight, to get enough movement, to drink enough water, to eat fresh greens, etc., yet this is how we were made! And this is what we are, as an aligned body."

"It's ridiculous," I continued in trance. "Would you ever think of an Indian holy man not being outside or dancing among the flowers?

"I mean, it's absurd that we put ourselves sort of in straight jackets, in dark little rooms, and then say, 'What's the matter? What's the matter?' [We] take medicine and go, 'What's wrong?'

"Yet when we think of holy people or . . . I mean, the thought of, say, Jesus—putting Him in an office somewhere in front of a computer eight to ten hours a day. It's like Clark Kent—you *know* that he's in disguise! The real Superman is flying through the universe.

"So it seems as if it's taking all this time to live a natural lifestyle, but it really isn't, because this is what matters—the alignment with true purpose.

"And with allowing—not just accepting, but *allowing* (in the sense of allowing into our cells and bones)—that God is supreme, is the Creator. So the walk in the sunlight, moving the arms over the shoulders, is actually a form of prayer. It's a prayer that for years, and throughout the world, people have done every day."

Evidently we had misunderstood Christ's commandment to love God with all our heart and mind and soul. To us this meant to attend church, pray, mediate, and have enlightening experiences. However, we were neglecting that God had also created nature and, specifically, the sun. Today we live our lives as if the natural world is optional since we have so many substitutes for it.

I was reminded that Jesus was thrown out of the temple and taught the multitudes outdoors. He also went into the wilderness for renewal. This was not a coincidence, just as His birth in the stable was not a coincidence. In addition, Muhammad had gone to the mountain and Buddha had sat under a tree.

Those of us who live in the modern world have separated ourselves from God by living as if we no longer need nature. Because we light our nights with electricity, heat our homes with the flick of a switch and get unlimited amounts of food on supermarket shelves, we are under the illusion that we, not God, are in control, little realizing that we would perish if it were not for sun, rain, earth, plants, and animals.

The sun is part of the natural world, and although we long for en-"light"-enment, we take sunlight totally for granted. Even though the purpose of our spiritual searching is to bring us to "light" from darkness, we have little respect for the one and only source of enduring light available to us: the sun.

However, we do not have to return to a primitive way of life to change our attitudes. I was told that all we had to do was to regularly greet the rising sun with our arms upraised, saying, "God is greater." Evidently, by doing this exercise we would eventually know our true place in the universe.

I was also told that we should spend at least 30 minutes outdoors every day in natural unfiltered sunlight. "It's important to have the light enter the eyes without lenses," I said, "without contacts or glasses."

This doesn't mean to stare at the sun—that can cause blindness. It means that we should simply be outside in natural sunlight, without glasses or contact lenses, every day. The minimum time is 30 minutes, but 60 minutes or longer is even better.

During the wintertime, the noon hour is best for absorbing sunlight through the eyes and the skin. During the summertime, when the sunlight is more intense, ten in the morning is best.

"What hampers the alignment is at the pineal," I said.

"And the body needs the natural material . . . raw material to do that with. It doesn't need a fluorescent light because that light is unbalanced. It doesn't need the glasses because they hold back most of the light and also [hold back] the oxygen content with contacts."

I saw a picture that looked like a textbook diagram. The eyes, facing right, were drawn in yellow against a black background, with a white line curved from each eye rising to the pineal gland above and behind them. The diagram showed how sunlight unlocked the pineal's connection with our soul.

The pineal is one of the seven glands corresponding to the chakras that raise the Light energy, or kundalini, within the body during prayer, meditation, and mystical experiences. Symbolically, the diagram showed how sunlight unlocked the pineal's connection with our soul.

Until approximately 30 years ago, the pineal was considered a vestigial organ, similar to the appendix, left over from our evolutionary past. However, recent scientific research has shown that the pineal is the source of the hormone melatonin, which is touted as a natural sleeping pill, contraceptive, mood enhancer, and infection fighter. Supposedly it can even prolong life.

There is probably much more to be learned about the pineal. While doing research, I read in Jacob Liberman's pioneering book *Light: Medicine of the Future* that although the pineal "is only the size of a pea, its functions are vast. It acts as the body's light meter, receiving light-activated information from the eyes, through the hypothalamus, and then sending out hormonal messages that have a profound effect on the mind and body."

Throughout the hypnosis sessions I had been told that the way to heal my overweight was through my eyes. Of course this made no sense to me at the time.

However, as I learned more about the pineal, I could see that healing of the body, through the soul, could occur at the pineal in the presence of sunlight. "The alignment [of the soul with the physical body] starts at the top of the chakras, instigated by the association of the pineal with sunlight and aligns all the way down. It's like a cloth that starts at the hood, and then the rest of the garment pastes itself against the back of the body and against the spine.

"The pineal has a little electric box in there that needs the sunlight. It's like the sunlight is a key to the pineal.

"The eyes are part of the electrical system in the body," I said while hypnotized, "so the reason why the sight is important isn't only for seeing clearly. It has to do with the electrical system [in the body and] . . . actually the alignment of the soul-body with the rest of the body."

We say that the eyes are the "windows of the soul." I was learning that the eyes were literally a window for sunlight to the soul via the pineal. And what else is the soul but light?

I was surprised that the information that I was supposed to convey was so specific and so physical. But I was also delighted that the suggestions were so relatively easy to do. Just about anybody, whether they live in a big city or in the country, can spend at least 30 minutes outdoors in the morning and greet the rising sun saying, "God is greater."

8

The Light Without

I had a lot to think about and a lot of time in which to think as I lay on the living room sofa with my foot swathed in ice packs elevated above my heart. Because the ankle had been previously injured, it took a long time to heal. As I hobbled along on crutches, carrying all my weight on one foot, my back began to hurt more and more. There were nights when I could hardly sleep. The doctor explained that the sacro-ileac joint over the weight-bearing leg had loosened. Now I had a bad back as well as an injured ankle.

Three times a week I went for physio- and later aqua-therapy. In addition, I always had to wear a special belt around my hips to hold the sacro-ileac joint tight.

As I lay on the couch thinking, the memory of the hypnosis sessions was very fresh. I was especially intrigued with the statement that the root of our undoing was that we live our lives as if we are greater than God and that the antidote was to greet the rising sun saying, "God is greater," three times.

I decided that even though I could hardly walk, I could manage to start each new day by going outside without my glasses and greeting the rising sun. Therefore, every morning I followed the same routine. Setting my alarm to ring a half hour before sunrise, I'd rouse myself out of bed, moving slowly to avoid the movements that hurt my back the most.

It was wintertime. I shuffled out onto the deck and waited, my breath billowing in mists around me. A sepulcher gray overshadowed the neighborhood. No one stirred. Nothing moved except a few birds who flitted nervously from branch to branch in the semi-darkness.

I waited, breathing in the chilly morning air. A cloud at the horizon lightened. I shifted from foot to foot and huffed through mittens to my frigid fingers, then slid them back into the armpits of my down jacket. The sky changed from gray to lavender as clouds glowed pink. At the skyline a gleam of deepening peach spread upward.

Pulling my hands out from the warmth of my jacket, I held my mittened fists at chest level with anticipation. Then I saw it. The orange-red orb broke through the horizon. I stretched my arms over my head three times and murmured, "God is greater."

My morning ritual complete, I shuffled back into the warm house.

Broken in body and spirit, I was determined to faithfully fulfill this simple exercise and see where it led me. As I consistently started the day with "God is greater," I was surprised to discover my reaction to the phrase. It bothered me. Although I had been praying to God for most of my life, I had never really opened myself to how small and insignificant I was compared to the Creator. I didn't like it.

But as I continued, I had to admit that on some level I did think I was greater than God. It was as if, when my prayers were answered, I felt that God was my servant, doing for me whatever I wanted or felt I needed.

We have been taught since our earliest days that we are immensely important. Science tells us that the Earth is the only known place where we great humans can live. The Bible says that we have been created in God's image, implying that we are almost equal to God. When I thought of the billions of people on Earth, all thinking they are the center of the universe, my mind boggled.

It was wintertime, the trees bare of leaves. I mimicked their branches reaching up for the sky. In my enthusiasm to grasp this concept, I cajoled my husband and children to pose for photographs in which they raised their arms as the sun rose. Kindly they humored me. I even took photos of myself, using the timer on my camera and a tripod.

When I developed my roll of film, my picture said it all. In the photograph there was a flick of light-colored cloth peeking out from below my winter jacket. It took me a while to figure out what that patch of cloth was. It turned out it was the tag on the special belt I had to wear to hold together my loose sacro-ileac joint.

I looked at that picture, thinking how I couldn't even walk without pain, and I knew how small and insignificant I really was. How could I think I was so special when I couldn't even make myself well? I couldn't make myself slender. I couldn't make myself taller or younger, or even change the color of my hair roots.

One morning as I stood on my deck greeting the rising sun, I looked around at the sleeping homes in my subdivision and thought how I was only one little person among hundreds in my neighborhood. Then I thought of all the cities and nations throughout the Earth and felt so much like a bee in a beehive or an ant in an anthill.

I thought how really gigantic the sun is compared to the Earth. And to think, there are hundreds of billions of suns that shine as stars in the night sky. Many of these suns probably have planetary systems. In addition, many of the stars that look like suns are actually far distant galaxies—collections of billions of stars. And some force created it all.

Here I was, like an ant among billions of ants, on a tiny anthill called Earth, having the audacious thought that I was somehow greater than the Creator of all this cosmos.

I felt very, very small. I hardly breathed. I let the feeling sink into me, tasting it, letting the fear of my insignificance settle. Standing on my frozen deck, alone, my breath misting around me, I waited, almost expecting the force of my nothingness to annihilate me.

But it didn't. I was still me. And I was OK. In fact, I was flooded by a wonderful feeling of warmth and happiness. I felt love, compassion, and community for all the other people in the Earth, in my neighborhood, in the wilderness, on the farms, and in all the cities and countries throughout the world.

Ironically, when I felt it in my bones that God was greater than me, it became much easier to love my neighbor as myself. We are all similarly very, very small. Even the greatest among us is very, very small compared to the sun and the cosmos. Even the least among us is no smaller than the rest of us compared to the immensity of Creation.

The paradox was that when I allowed the terrifying feeling to surface—that I was really not very important, and certainly almost nothing compared to God—I derived peace from it.

And then I became happy. Happy that the sun shone on me, that the rain fell, that the breeze rustled the pine needles above me. And I felt community and compassion for all the other little beings on this planet with me.

The more I affirmed that God was greater than me, the more I felt my proper place—small, insignificant, but definitely a part—in all of God's creations. I belonged. I was part of this marvelous, wonderful, fantastic whole, the cosmos. I had a place in it. I felt an immense peace in this realization.

My idea of the sun also changed. I began to look forward to seeing it every day. Would the sunrise be orange or pink? Would there be clouds in front, below, above, or beside it?

Eventually, the sun became like a being—powerful, life-giving, benevolent—our protector with a soul and a personality. The image of each morning's sunrise would stay with me throughout the day, lighting my dismal, frustrating moments. I would see it again, rising in my mind—the memory of that day's dawn— available to me whenever I needed cheering.

I discovered that the sun is like a counterpart to the Light I experience during meditation. Whereas the Light within belongs to my unconscious, the sun belongs to my conscious mind. It is the Light without.

9

The Dark Force

I was troubled. According to the vision, I was supposed to write a history of the soul on Earth. I could see how my first lifetime on Earth would be a good starting point. However, it bothered me because it appeared that sex with the beast had caused my entrapment in the physical. Could something as beautiful and natural as sex, something that almost every animal, insect, and flower participated in—the act that made the next generation—could this have really caused the "fall?"

I made another appointment with Lynn. She agreed with me that the story reminded her of Genesis. Like the tale of Adam and Eve, there is a temptation and a banishment. There is also a change from bliss to separation and shame. Before the Fall, the light beam was connected with the Creator and knew its purpose in existence: exploration.

Moreover, the light beam knew no sorrow. There were no opposites, there was no good or evil. It was all simply different vibrations. There was no judgment that one type of vibration was better or worse than another.

The change seemed to occur at the time that the light beam encountered the ape-like beast and indulged in sexual play, albeit as a cloud. At the same time, the senses began to operate. The wisp-of-smoke being listened for footsteps and saw stars. The sensate world appeared to be coupled with the world of opposites. It was like the Buddhist creation story, which says that we separated from God into a world of duality.

Although it seemed that participation in sexual vibrations had caused the situation of duality, when I closely reviewed the tape, I realized that the change had actually occurred earlier. The Light Being began to dim at the time when it began to experiment with going deeper into the vibrations, no longer merely dancing on them. At that time the perceptions began to differentiate into the ape-like being and the tree, in other words, the sensate world.

So was it the sex that caused the fall from grace or something else? Whatever it was, the wisp-of-smoke being was certainly ashamed of whatever it had done.

Lynn and I decided to go back to find out. Since this was the incident that had apparently caused my present obesity, Lynn said she was going to use a technique that would clear the shame and change the past.

When I was sufficiently in trance, she asked me to find the time of change from light beam to amber translucent being on my time line. I was to float above it.

When I was floating in the Light, right above the place where I was enjoying the vibrations with the beast, Lynn told me to ask my unconscious mind what I could learn from the awareness of being at this crucial place of change.

To my surprise, I found myself in a struggle. Bouncing from right to left and around from the waist up, I fought with something or someone. Flip, flop, right to left and around and around. It wasn't a person or even a being. It was an energy. It was without outline and was constantly changing shape like an ameba. It was dark and it was strong. It grasped me, trying to pull me down, right down to the bottom of a long funnel that extended from the Light down to the line that represented time. It felt like a life and death struggle.

"What is the dark thing?" asked Lynn. "Get to know it a little better." I hesitated. I was pretty sure I knew what the dark force was. However, I really did not want to say it out loud or even acknowledge it because it was terrifying to think that I was locked in combat with a force so powerful. I was afraid. No, I was terrified.

I was aware that the first time I had struggled with this dark power, I had lost. Because of losing that battle, I was now trapped in the physical and unable to go home. As so often happened in the hypnosis, when I had difficulty facing the events my unconscious presented, I saw the answer as floating words.

"My mind says, 'Satan.'" There was a long pause as my conscious mind went through convolutions of revulsion and fear. "It laughs," I exclaimed in distress. It was laughing a deep, exultant laugh as if it enjoyed capturing me.

"And what is the dark thing trying to do with or to you?" asked Lynn.

"Swallow me," I replied.

"But it can't, can it?" asked Lynn.

I thought that was extremely presumptuous of Lynn. It seemed as if it definitely was about to swallow me. I had to assume that Lynn knew what she was doing. I was very glad that she was both experienced and competent.

"Well," I answered apprehensively, "it keeps laughing like it's going to." However, after a while I seemed to gain some ground. "I'm overpowering the dark thing," I said. "It feels so good to overpower it!"

As I continued to struggle, I gained further ground. "I've gotten the dark form below me," I said. "That's where I want it to stay. It's not laughing as loud because I've stepped on it." I had pushed the dark form down with my left heel and leapt out of its grasp.

I laughed joyously. I was free. "Hah! I bruise my heel on it!" I exclaimed. Then, I remembered how I had just recently bruised my left heel when I broke off the bone chip and tendon.

In the hypnosis I was relieved to see that I shoved the dark force down with my left foot. Even though I bruised my heel on it, I was able to leave it below and ascend into the top part of the funnel, into the Light.

I had always thought that the Genesis story of the temptation by the serpent was merely an allegorical story about temptation. Now I was reliving an experience in which the serpent was only allegorical in the sense that it stood for the dark force, which I called Satan.

Interestingly, the symbology of the bruised heel also occurs in the Bible. This has to do with the prophecy, in Isaiah, of the Christ's birth in which it was foretold that a virgin would give birth to a child who would crush the serpent that had caused the original fall from grace. In crushing the serpent, the Savior would bruise His heel.

What a coincidence! I was in the process of healing the event that had caused my own Fall and had coincidentally bruised my heel just before this session. My heel was so badly bruised that it looked like it was in a black cast.

Could it be that we have all fought with the dark force—and lost—resulting in our entrapment in the physical? Could it be that the story of Adam and Eve is *our* story as well?

Under hypnosis I told Lynn that the funnel signified a great change that stretched through all time. It had "funneled" me into my entrapment in the physical.

Lynn asked me to lift far above the time line. "Now I'd like you to just allow the Light that you are so aware of now to flow into the you that is above the funnel," she said.

I felt amazingly loved while bathed in this pure Light. Lynn told me to allow this Light to fill me with a sense of infinite and divine love, healing, and transformation. I remembered that Lynn had told me at the beginning of this session that we would change my past. I realized that we were at that point when I would be healed.

"Let that Light begin pouring forth from your heart," Lynn said, "down through that funnel to the much earlier you in the time line, and notice what that does to that darkness."

I told Lynn that I hadn't even known the darkness yet. I was so healed that I hadn't encountered it, and I didn't even know it existed.

"Good," said Lynn. "Just fill and surround that you in the time line in that beautiful body . . ."

"No," I interrupted, "it's before my body . . . <u>the body came from knowing the dark</u>."

This was interesting to me because it meant that the wisp-of-smoke was an actual body. However, the light beam was not.

"OK," said Lynn. "Fill the you that is pre-corporeal totally with the Light now."

I did. Lynn told me to move forward a little bit on the line that represented time and to notice what happened when I was given the gift of a physical form with which to explore the Earth.

<u>I replied that I now had humility</u>. I said that I could see how I had split the humility from me. It had floated away while I was still in the vibrational state, before I became trapped in the physical. This had made me vulnerable to Satan's power. Then the dark power had swallowed me and pulled me down into the physical.

So that's what had caused the Fall. <u>Because I didn't want only to explore, I wanted also to experience, I had separated myself from the humility</u> that kept me within God's will.

It wasn't the sex.

It was the lack of humility that had caused my Fall. True, the desire to experience sexual vibrations had tempted me to split off the humility. But it wasn't the sex, per se. <u>It was disobedience—the original sin</u>.

It made sense. It was the same problem Christ had had . . . and I assume with which we all suffer. Disobedience. His whole lifetime had been about obedience. He had been tempted by the devil but remained inviolate. It wasn't until He had resisted the temptations of Satan that He came into His full glory and rightful destiny. Then, at the prime of His life, the apex of His power, when multitudes of thousands followed Him to hear His words, He was told He would now die. He prayed to God in the wilderness, "Take this cup from Me," but in the end He remained obedient to God's will with "Nonetheless, Thy will be done."

And He allowed God's will to be done in Him—allowing Himself to be crucified. Here was the paradox of the power of the unconscious. By letting go of His own personal will and doing God's will, Jesus became stronger. He was able to overcome death and was resurrected.

Over and over, the theme of the first book of the Bible, Genesis, seems to be obedience to God's will. Adam and Eve are thrown out of the Garden of Eden because they don't obey God. The issue doesn't seem to be the fruit of the tree, the serpent, or who took the first bite. The point of the story is that they were told not to eat the fruit of this tree and they disobeyed. Then they suffered the consequences.

In any case, once I reclaimed my humility under hypnosis and made myself whole again, my perception of my predicament changed. I was no longer discouraged. I no longer wailed, "I want to go home."

In fact, I danced. I saw myself begin to spin to the right with my arms raised up to the sky, in the same position I had been told to greet the morning sun. I floated. The spin started slowly and felt as controlled as a planet spinning around a sun.

"And concerning that desire eventually to go home" asked Lynn, "what do you know in this body about going home?"

"It's inevitable."

"Feel that joy in your body," said Lynn, "and claim your body now. Embrace your body with love. Acknowledge it as the God-given gift it is."

I saw myself transcending the funnel that stretched through all time. I rose out of the funnel. I was free. "I want to know where I'm going," I said.

"Just go up and take a peek," said Lynn.

I went up above the time line and looked out into the future. There I saw something I'd dreamt about once. I looked like an Amazon, a female warrior, with short billowing silver hair and buccaneer boots. My body was gorgeous, tall, slender, and strong. I was a star-being holding three worlds by the reins. We careened through space in a large orbit surrounded by stars, galaxies, and nebulae. The worlds were beautiful, strong, and vital. So was I, and I cared for and controlled these worlds so they worked in unison. They were held by reins, as three horses would be held in the traditional Russian sleigh called a troika. I carried a whip that represented Light rather than pain. It cracked with inspiration, exaltation, and joy. It was as if I could feel the energy among the three heavenly bodies and knew how to control them so they worked harmoniously.

Although the scenario appeared fantastic, it was not so farfetched when taken in the context of a Light Being whose mission was to explore the universe. The Light Being's potential future was to evolve into a star-being.

One morning, months after this session, as I continued to greet the rising sun, saying, "God is greater," I was flooded with the realization that the sun, which had become a benevolent protector and friend, was actually an image of my real self. If I truly was a Light Being, as I remembered myself to be, then, when I looked at the sun, I was actually looking at an image of my real self.

**I realized that the sun represented
my real self, a Light Being.**

10

The Light Force

Whether I liked it or not, I was learning a history of the soul I could tell the Golden Ones, the young people who would be bringing in the Fifth Root Race. It appeared that we had originally been created in God's image as pure Light and Love. As such, we had truly been citizens of the universe, able to travel from star system to star system, called "aliens" today on Earth. We had made the mistake of separating ourselves from humility, thereby making us vulnerable to a dark force which imprisoned us in the physical. We wanted desperately to go "home" to oneness with God.

In my next session with Lynn, I would unwittingly discover some of the things we have to do to return to Oneness. It was December 21, 1995, four days before Christmas. Lynn and I thought we were going to explore my purpose in life. And we did. But we also somehow found ourselves again in a wonderland.

When my body and conscious mind were thoroughly relaxed, Lynn gave me the mental "address" of this particular session: ". . . *become more and more in tune with that purpose that has brought you into being.*"

I'm sure that Lynn meant "brought you (Carole) into being (in this lifetime)"; however, I can only assume that my unconscious interpreted this statement to mean "that brought you, *in your essence*, into being *for eternity.*"

As before, Lynn brought me to the Light. From the Light, I was to go to a special sanctuary, a place of learning and spiritual instruction "where you can meet those whose whole purpose is to guide, direct, to help you any way that you may need help to fulfill your highest purpose."

I saw high white mountains with pointed peaks. The sky was very blue. I was on the tallest of the mountains on a steep but gently curving path to the top. There were small white desert-type plants and rocks on either side of the path.

Up above I saw a cave in the summit which was open like a round window. Looking out through this stone "window" there were three shaven-headed men, in robes similar to those worn by Tibetan Lamas except that these robes were white.

They were wise men, neither happy nor sad, but rather stern-faced with kind, wise eyes. They looked out over the planet from the white mountain at the top of the world.

There was a small entranceway to the cave on the right side of the peak. An intense white-gold light emanated through the opening. The path I was on led right up to it. I went in.

Inside I found a pure white oval chamber with a high domed ceiling. The atmosphere within the room was perfectly comfortable, neither too hot nor too cold, but very fresh.

The Christ was there with me in the entrance passageway. He was my dear friend, glad that I had sought Him out. Because He looked like various paintings I'd seen of Him, with wispy brown hair, I suspect that this image was my mind's representation of the Christ spirit or the Christ Consciousness. It was the oneness with this Christ spirit that had made Jesus the Christ.

However, I was curious to know if I had lived during the time that Jesus of Nazareth was in the Earth. At the end of the French Revolution lifetime, as I knelt at the guillotine to be executed, the guillotine had become a cross. It seemed then as if I was reliving the Crucifixion. Therefore I now asked, "I would like to know something about what my experience was with Christ when He was alive."

"Does He show you anything?" asked Lynn.

I found myself in a cave in the wilderness with a number of other people. It was very hot outside. We were in the cave because it was shaded and cooler. Through the narrow doorway of the cave, which was built into the side of a hill or cliff, I could see hot dry brown hills.

"We are also in the cave in the wilderness because we are safe here," I said. "Jesus is a hunted man. Those in power are threatened by the things He says and does, especially since He is gaining a following. They are afraid they may lose power, and so they want to kill Him."

Inside the cave some of us were sitting on short three-legged wooden stools along both sides of a narrow room. Jesus sat among those on the right. I was on my knees with a pan of water. I had just washed His feet and had wiped them dry with my long, thick, dark hair. I kissed His feet.

"I love Him deeply. There's also a sense of sadness, as if I must express this deep love in the best way I know how—now. It is a very solemn moment because He has just told us He must leave us soon. I don't want Him to leave. But He says He must. And He kisses my feet. I start to cry."

One section of the cave was covered up with boards. Pencil-thin streams of sunlight peeked through the cracks. It appeared to be a kitchen. There were two or three women there who were whispering among themselves.

This was the time that He said that the greatest among us is servant of all and that we must do as He does. And so He washed our feet.

There was a young man with shoulder-length straight dark hair sitting on a three-legged stool along the left wall of the room. The young man folded his arms and turned away from Jesus, muttering something to the effect that he wouldn't let his friend wash his feet. He pressed himself against the wall, his arms crossed and his feet as far away from Jesus as he could get them.

I noticed how sinewy the upper arms of this dark-haired young man were. As I relived this memory, I thought how all the paintings of the apostles made them look so ponderous and bulky, whereas this young man, who I know is called a disciple by our present church, was neither ponderous nor bulky but a wiry, intense young man. He was one of Jesus' close friends, perhaps a cousin.

I looked at the sinewy muscles in this young man's upper arms and knew he had been hauling fish nets since he was a boy. He was a hard-working, hands-on type of person, dependable, knowledgeable about the sea, and a real and true friend.

The men were young—much younger than any of the paintings of the apostles I'd ever seen. Furthermore, all the paintings I'd ever seen of Christ, the apostles and Mary had them swathed in voluminous fabric. But here, in this past life memory, they were clothed in a single, simple tunic of coarsely woven cloth, almost sleeveless, with a cord tied around the waist. In addition, I'd never seen paintings of them sweating. We were all dripping with sweat, from our hairlines down our faces.

I remarked to Lynn that Jesus' hair was a dark red-brown color, not the plain brown nor strawberry blonde I'd seen in paintings. Then I added, "But of course He was sweating so much, and we were in the cave, so his hair may have appeared darker than it really was."

Jesus walked on His knees, pulling the pan containing the water after Him, over to the dark-haired young man. As He crawled over, Jesus mumbled something to the effect of, "Just go along with it."

Another young man, with curly golden hair, sat on a three-legged stool behind the dark-haired young man. It was as if they were brothers or best friends. The blonde one entreated the dark one to submit, explaining something to him. Jesus then mumbled something to them.

I couldn't really hear what they were saying because my head was spinning—I couldn't understand why my beloved friend and teacher was leaving us. It tore at my heart.

Then Jesus just lifted the dark-haired young man's feet and put them in the water. He didn't argue; He simply did it. I could see that He was distressed, although He was doing a pretty good job of hiding it.

After the crucifixion, I understood that Jesus was in anguish because He felt He hadn't had enough time to teach us everything, and He knew He would be killed soon.

So, He did the one thing that He felt would best illustrate what He was trying to tell us. By washing our feet, He showed the most outstanding quality that made Him One with the Creator: humility.

"We're all sad," I said, sobbing, "but He isn't. He loves us! I just have this memory, this sense of me looking down at His head while He's washing my feet and kissing me. I touch His head . . . and I'm crying."

The next memory was at the Crucifixion. "I'm standing back and the crowds are there and He's on the cross and I can't even cry because we'd be killed," I sighed. "We just stand there. And I can't stand the pain, and I see Him and . . ."

"Do you make any promises, any vows, in this moment?" interjected Lynn.

"That I would follow Him to the ends of the Earth. And that I would take that pain also."

"And have you made good on that promise?" asked Lynn.

"Certainly, as to the pain [referring to the French Revolution]."

11

The Life to Come

Now that the past life memory of my life with Jesus was over, Lynn told me to let Him take me to a very special place—the place where I could view the main events of the life that was to come. I found myself back in the high-ceilinged cave at the summit of the white mountain on top of the world. This Christ, representative of the Christ Consciousness, looked more symbolic, like a painting, with light brown hair, glowing with a soft aura.

I found myself standing in front of a white lectern in the place where the three holy men had stood. I felt humble, young, quiet, and still, a short female figure clothed in a simple white garment with short sleeves, with a white cord around my waist. The garment, which hung to a length between my knees and ankles, was constructed of one piece of fabric. My body was small and delicate, my hair its normal dark color but cut very simply and bluntly to just below ear level. I stood there, my arms hanging at my sides, my head bowed slightly.

The Christ stood flush behind me. He was taller than me, so His head was above mine. We were as close to One as possible in physical bodies. We both stepped forward on our right feet. Our left feet were behind us. He held my right hand strongly in His right hand and put it, with His, on the lectern.

He was totally and completely supporting me. It occurred to me that He was plastered against my spine as if the kundalini, the energy that rises up through the spiritual centers in meditation, was bathed in the Christ Consciousness. Even His head, which hovered over mine, was like the East Indian hooded cobra that symbolizes the kundalini.

However, during the hypnosis, I was not thinking, "This is the Christ energy rising, kundalini-like, up my spine." To me, it was Christ, my beloved friend, helping me to look at my life.

With Him superimposed behind me, I was amazed by His unconditional love for me and cried softly because of it.

From the lectern, I could look out at the world via the same oval window through which the three holy men had gazed. In front of us was the view of the white mountains and the blue sky. I could see, swirling in blues, green, whites, and yellows, scenes which symbolized my life.

At first I heard the word "upheavals," followed by a sense of upheavals in the Earth.

I didn't know if this meant the "earth" of my own body or our planet, "Earth."

Then I heard, "Have no fear. I am with you."

I saw a green grassy field, a field I had been seeing since the beginning of this part of the session. At first I didn't know what it meant, but then I had a flash of comprehension that one thing it meant was growth.

There was a long, long pause as I tried to assimilate what I was hearing. I felt stunned. I heard the Christ say something that was unbelievable and frightening. I didn't like what I was hearing.

"Carole, you are my beloved, and you will not be here at the end of the 20th century.'"(I'm writing this in October 1999 and, so far, I'm still here. There is more on this later in the chapter.)

Amazingly, after crying because of Christ's great love for me, I was not crying for myself now. Because I was hypnotized, there was no remorse over losing my body, which was asleep during the hypnosis. My unconscious mind would obviously survive the death of the body.

I asked to know what would happen. There was another very long pause. Again I had so much to assimilate. I heard that He would take me with Him. My mind reeled in disbelief.

I heard, "I will gather the faithful—I will gather them to Me."

There was another long, long pause. I sighed. I might believe in Jesus the Christ as the Son of God, and I might enjoy reading about Him in the Bible. However, to me the Second Coming was something figurative. It meant that more and more of us would turn to God or the Light within as we realized our man-made world did not provide all the answers. But here I was finding out it was, or it might be, a real incident that could happen to me.

"I think we're going out the gate," I said. I saw Christ gathering people to Himself. We were dancing in that slow turning dance I had experienced after uniting with the humility in the previous session. We danced toward the lighted-up place on the hill that looked like swirling clouds—the place that would take me home. It was the Star Gate that would allow us to transcend time and leave this planetary system.

"I need to know what I have to do," I said.

In answer I was told that I would have to make my body whole, correct, healthy, including my eyes, which didn't seem possible because I've been near-sighted and wearing glasses since I was six years old. However, I had the sense that the exercises in the sunlight, described in Chapter Seven, God is Greater, would help to cure my sight.

It appeared that the Christ was telling me that once I was whole in body, totally aligned with the Light that was my real self, ". . . we will dance to the gate."

I wanted to know what "home," the place where we were going to, was like. I saw colors and felt vibrations and knew immediately what it meant—the end of duality and the world of the senses. We would be free of the physical.

I wondered why we would want to free ourselves of the physical. "Evolution," I replied. This was not the type of survival-of-the-fittest animal evolution that is usually referred to here on Earth. It was the evolution of the soul, the Light Being we are in essence. (The evolution of the physical, in which we are entrapped, has its own path through the nature kingdom.)

Our liberation from the physical was not evolution but an escape to freedom. After we became free, thereby transcending duality, we could leave via the Star Gate, free to roam the universe and continue our soul evolution.

I could now understand how a light beam, whose mission was exploration, could evolve into a star-being capable of controlling worlds.

I asked what I should do in the meanwhile. I also heard again, as I had when learning how to make God greater in my life, to take *seriously being outdoors, exercising, eating right*—to take all of that really seriously.

And then I was told ". . . to give away as much as possible of things I know. Then just to keep giving, to be like a funnel: *to give. I have the sense* [to give] *'til there's nothing left of me . . .*"

Nothing left of me? It seemed as if my goal was to become nothing.

In Gary R. Renard's 2002 book, *The Disappearance of the Universe*, Renard shows how we are really nothing and that our concept of being something is merely an illusion. He also says that when we accept again that we are nothing, we will experience indescribable bliss, which was my experience as a First Root Race being.

In the hypnosis session I continued by saying that once there would be nothing left of me, ". . . somehow I'll be free then. There's the sense that it doesn't really matter what, as long as I'm giving the most of what I have."

The implication was, of course, that knowledge was all that I really had from my earth experiences. All the things we thought we owned, such as clothes, houses, land, businesses, food, jewelry, cars, plants, trees, even people—children, spouses, employees, etc.—were only in relationship with us.

I was told that writing, or anything that reached large masses of people like television or movies, would be good, as well as helping women and children.

Then I became afraid. I said to the Christ, "I don't want to go." He replied that that wasn't right, that I shouldn't be afraid.

To encourage me, He filled me with His Light and Love. I felt like I was bursting with a resplendent light. He also assured me that I wasn't crazy, which was really reassuring, because by now I was beginning to wonder.

It seemed as if, as in the Bible, people would just be taken, as in "the Rapture." As an example, I saw myself working in the garden. It was a beautiful sunny day. The garden looked great. I was slender and healthy. Although I wasn't wearing glasses, I could see every little flower and bee in the garden clearly.

As I straightened up from working with a row of green plants, my arms raised in that turning dance I had experienced in the previous session. I began to shimmer, changing into pure Light. I no longer existed as a human being.

As the shimmer began, I was filled with joy and became aware of the Christ, Jesus, my dear friend, there with me. We began to slowly turn, floating upward, dancing to the gate, which I saw again as swirling lighted clouds in the sky. It was as if the swirling lighted clouds were an actual address in the sky. There were others dancing with us to the gate.

At the end of the session, Lynn told me to ask the Christ anything else that I needed to know for the immediate future that would give me a sense of guidance and direction in doing His will.

I saw myself in a totally blue place. I knelt on one knee, my head bowed. These strange words appeared: "*Rabboni ashmae-un, tah.*" I have no idea what these sounds meant. For all I know, they're gibberish. However, when I said them, they seemed to mean, "Beloved Teacher, how would You want me to emulate You, to follow You?"

He placed His right hand on my head and replied, "Feed My sheep," which had the sense of meaning to "just give out to everyone."

I heard my reply as, *"Mae un t-hah nae"* (with an aspirate "h," I explained to Lynn), which supposedly meant, "Yes, of course." Or that it doesn't really matter what I do as long as I just give out.

Then I became distressed. I said, "I accept. I must accept this." I was panicked. This was too outrageous. What did I know about feeding His sheep? How could this be real? The Second Coming? What was going on? Was this some kind of a joke? I couldn't do it. All I wanted was a normal life, with my family, my garden, my friends, and a thin body.

What was going on? Then I assured myself that I could accept it in the unconscious but consciously it would take awhile.

I became aware of a very deep guilt I was carrying, as if I had caused His crucifixion. Then I remembered that I had heard Him say in church, "I died for you."

I realized that the guilt came from being one of the beings He had come here to free. If I had not become stuck in the physical, He would not have had to go through this for us. I had seen how He suffered for us on the Cross, especially with the jeering, scorning, ridiculing crowd, and I felt devastated that I had caused it in any way, because I loved Him so much.

12

Love of the Physical

During the weeks following this session, I was overwhelmed with the memory of returning to the vibrational state and going out the Star Gate with the Christ. Instead of being happy about it, however, I was extremely distressed. I didn't want to leave the physical. I didn't want to lose my senses.

Every sunset, every gracefully arching tree brought tears to my eyes. I was a photographer. Every color, every nuance, every shape was pregnant with beauty and wonder for me. Especially when I looked at trees with their branches raised in honor of the light, I cried. How could I leave this behind?

I heard birds singing, the surf pounding on the shore, water burbling into a storm sewer after a rain, and a baby's cry. I listened to fantastic classical and rock music filled with joy, power, and yearning, and especially to those songs that are so inspiring they make you feel like you're soaring over the mountain tops.

How could I live without these? The smell of the earth, a wood fire, an orange, fresh air, laundry dried in sunlight, the fragrance of honeysuckle, a rose, the taste of my favorite foods, the feel of the wind, the touch of my husband, a hug from my children, would all be lost to me.

I wondered, should I tell my family about this session? The Second Coming was such a remote possibility. They might be upset for no reason. And it seemed so unlikely that I would ever be nearly perfect in body.

In the middle of all of this, Clair and I went shopping at the grocery store. She had been home from college for the Christmas holidays, and we needed to purchase the many foodstuffs, toiletry items, and stationery supplies she'd need when she went back to live in the dorm her second semester.

As we walked out of the grocery store into the parking lot, she pushed the shopping cart ahead of me. There was a slight downward slope in the pavement. The weight of all our purchases sent the grocery cart coasting down the slope. Instead of grabbing the cart as I would have done, Clair took a flying leap onto the back of the cart and took a ride, as she had done so many times when she was young.

In an instant I saw the white-blonde hair of her childhood mix with the dark blonde hair of her adolescence. I could hear the delighted giggle of her younger days mix with the fullness of her mature delight. She was still the same beautiful little girl, but so much older—a woman now.

I thought, You won't be able to ride the cart like that when you're pregnant.

And then it hit me. What if I wasn't here when Clair was pregnant? What if I didn't see her belly swollen with life? What if I couldn't listen to her joy, complaints, fascination, know-it-allness when she was expecting? What if I didn't see my beloved Clair holding her cherished little baby in her arms? Her little one at her breast? Her husband supporting them, filled with pride, feeling the strength of his manhood manifest in the lives he now cared for and protected? What if I wouldn't be here for all that?

Oh God, how I wanted to be with my children forever. I didn't want to leave. I loved the Earth. I loved my family. I wanted to stay here, reincarnating with them over and over again in different roles. Even if we all left together, we would no longer have emotional interactions without our bodies.

I decided I would have to tell my children just in case the Second Coming really did happen to me. This might be terrible news for them because they had already lost their father to kidney cancer. One by one, privately, I would tell them. It would be so unkind, should it really happen, to leave them bewildered.

After Clair had been settled into the dorm for a month or so, I decided to tell her. By then most of the emotion had been wrung out of me.

We sat in the study lounge. Because it was early in the day, we were the only ones there. Somehow the subject of my writing came up. I began to tell her about the Second Coming.

"Cool," she said. "So what else?"

"They're going out the gate," I replied. "Remember, there's supposed to be this Star Gate where you can get out of the Earth's planetary system?"

"Yeah, I remember, like that movie Star Gate."

"Sort of. But when we go out the gate, we'll be back in the vibrational mode. We won't have bodies anymore, so we won't have the senses. Our experiences won't be organized into sense impressions. Do you know what I mean?"

"Yeah. A fly's eyes have so many lenses that everything it sees is like a kaleidoscope. Dog's see in black and white and are near-sighted. Cats see in the dark. We know our world by the type of sensory organs we have."

"That's right. Well, when we go out the gate, we won't have sensory organs. We'll be pure Light. We'll no longer see or hear or smell or touch. It'll be like it was before we got stuck in matter. Everything will be different vibrations, and we won't experience them as separate from us—they'll be in and through and around us."

Clair could see I was sad. "Mom, you're one of them."

"Well, that's what the hypnosis said, but I think it was just to show me how it's a possibility for all of us."

We looked at each other. I took a deep breath. "The trouble is that it's still so fresh. It seems like it might really happen. I didn't want to tell you."

"Mom, I'm grown up now. Dad couldn't say good-bye to anyone when he was dying. If you knew about this ahead of time and never said good-bye or how much you loved me, I'd never forgive you."

I got the joke, smiled and then felt the sting of tears in my eyes. I took another deep breath and smiled through the tears. "It's a possible future," I said sniffling.

We reached for each other and hugged. I felt Clair's delicate female frame in my arms, felt her ribs rise with her breathing, felt the smoothness of her face, smelled her hair, thought how there was once a time when she was so small that I could hold all of her on one arm, sitting in the rocking chair as she slept, a scrunched-up dark pink face swaddled in baby clothes, making little puppy sounds.

As we separated, I saw that her eyes glistened, too. Pulling a tissue out of my purse, I wiped my eyes and blew my nose. Clair stretched out her hand, and I rummaged in my purse for another tissue.

"Well, anyway, it doesn't seem likely because, supposedly, I have to heal myself—my eyesight, my hemorrhoids, my over-weight. I'm supposed to get enough sunlight, eat greens—you know, all that good stuff we're all supposed to do."

I found the right time and the right way to tell Adam, my oldest, and Miriam, my youngest, as well. John, as I expected, was concerned until he realized we were talking about some kind of a mystical event rather than a terminal illness. Then he didn't really hear another word I said.

13

Going Crazy

Meanwhile, although I had stopped gaining weight, I had a much bigger physical problem. My ripped tendon was not healing, probably because I'd ripped the same tendon years ago on my bicycle trip.

After a couple of months in which it became obvious that I was not going to regain my mobility anytime soon, I lost my job. NASA was making budget cuts, and our contract was ordered to cut a position. Since I could not be at work, mine was the obvious choice.

I wasn't too upset because, with my back hurting so much, I didn't think I would ever be able climb around wind tunnels again. Moreover, I had been so unhappy after the miscarriage, hormonal imbalance, and weight gain, that my heart hadn't been in my work anyway.

To my surprise, my employer had a very generous disability policy. Now I had the financial wherewithal to write and still care for my children.

It was uncanny how everything kept falling into place so I could fulfill the directive given me in my vision to "awaken the Golden Ones" and write a history of the soul on Earth. The day after our old unreliable home computer finally broke, the disability company called and offered me a lump sum payment. I would have enough money to purchase a new computer and even buy a printer! Until now I had had to hobble to the library with a disc to print a hard copy. I would also have enough money to keep my two older children in college.

However, although everything else was falling into place, I was not. To say that I was challenged by the information in the hypnosis sessions would be a definite understatement. I was terrified by it.

I was especially scared *because* everything kept falling into place.

It was like I was in the grip of something beyond my control.

Something was happening to me. I had dreamt about the man I would marry and then met him and married him. I had had a miscarriage, gained a lot of weight, and gone to a hypnotherapist. During a healing by angelic beings, I had been told that "further adjustments" would be made and within a week had fallen down the stairs and hurt my ankle and my back. Perhaps the fall down the stairs made the further adjustments. Also, just after I had "bruised" my physical heel in conscious waking life, I had "bruised" my heel while pushing Satan down in hypnosis.

While in trance, I had had a vision in which I was told that I was supposed to write a book to "awaken the Golden Ones." With the disability I now had the time and money with which to do so. Moreover, because of my injuries, I could hardly walk. Just about the only thing I *could* do was to stay home and write! You bet I was terrified.

I was equally afraid of *writing* the book as I was of *not* writing it. I was supposed to write that I was an alien—from Arcturus—this from a person who was embarrassed to cry in church. That I was really originally pure Light and then had changed into a wisp-of-smoke thought form. And that the Golden Ones were supposed to be bringing in the Fifth Root Race.

And this information was supposed to be an explanation of the Bible. Oh, did I mention that around this time I had a dream which said, "This is an explanation of the Bible"?

Going Crazy

I wondered if I was losing my mind. I cried, I railed, I poured out my anger to God in my prayers. John's face would betray panic as I would cry to him that "I do not want to write this stupid book—it's dumb, people will think I'm crazy, people will sneer at you at work, and the kids will be laughed at."

"Then don't write it," he'd say. "Write something else. Get some kind of job."

Then I'd lash out at him. "What, and have something else happen to me even worse? I thought you loved me. How could you think of something so awful?"

I know he wondered what was happening to me. His lovely new wife had first become a blimp, then a cripple, followed by her losing her job (with two kids in college), and now she appeared to be losing her mind.

John had his own way of handling this crisis. When my former work colleagues would ask him what I was doing now, he'd reply, "She's writing a book. It's fiction, but she thinks it's non-fiction." Perhaps he's right.

I talked a lot with Clair, who was home from college during that terrible summer. We discussed using a pseudonym so that no one would know the name of the crazy person who wrote the book. Clair reminded me of my sin of being wishy-washy.

We also toyed with totally rewriting the book as fiction. Under hypnosis I'd been told to write it as a cartoon. I had no idea what that meant. However, the next session on Atlantis certainly leant itself to a cartoon treatment. As far as I was concerned, it was a total joke.

It was one thing to write about being, in our essence, Light. But Atlantis? Most people I knew were firmly divided into two camps. They either considered the *possibility* that it had been a reality, or they believed unequivocally that it was bunk.

In my many radio interviews since the publication of *The Golden Ones*, I had discovered that the first question most of my radio hosts asked about Atlantis was, "Where is it?" And, of course, I didn't know the answer. No one knows. There are many theories. In fact, there have been many discoveries, both archeological and mythological, that support the researcher's ideas as to the location of that great island-nation. There have been many proposals. Some say that Ireland once was Atlantis. Others say Spain. Still others, the Mediterranean island of Cyprus or Spartel Island off the Straits of Gibraltar. Other researchers locate Atlantis as the Greek island of Santorini or even somewhere in the South China Sea.

Recently, a Canadian research team led by Paulina Zelitsky, found what may be manmade ruins off the coast of Cuba. Since there are also caves nearby with petroglyphs that some researchers believe show a cataclysmic destruction, there is speculation that these underwater ruins may be ruins of Atlantis.

Andrew Collins, author of *Gateway to Atlantis: The Search for the Source of a Lost Civilization*, agrees that Atlantis must have been in the Caribbean. In his 2002 book he explains his findings based on a study of the writings of the ancient Athenian philosopher Plato.

As it turns out, even in 355 BC when Plato wrote the *Timaeus* and *Critias*, our first written record of this great island-nation in the Atlantic Ocean, controversy raged over its existence. Plato's disciple Aristotle thought that Plato had made the whole story up.

Plato was a highly respected philosopher, and even today, over two millennia after he lived, we still revere his insights—except, for his "imaginings" on Atlantis. And I, an unknown, was going to write about a frog controlling a crystal in a tower in Atlantis? I thought not.

In Atlantis I had found myself to be, of all things, a frog-like being. I had green skin—which made me so embarrassed that I couldn't even admit it to Lynn—long sticky fingers, big dark eyes and a cute, but green, pixie face with a shock of black hair that fell over my forehead.

I was pretty sure that even among people who were open to reincarnation, I would be considered a weirdo. I could just see me at a "come-as-you-were" costume party:

"So what were you in a past life?"

"A frog."

"Oh."

Going Crazy

There weren't many people with whom I could discuss my experiences:

"So what'cha been doing with yourself lately?"

"Awakening the Golden Ones."

"Oh."

I tried to tell my friends:

"So I hear you've been writing a book. What's it about?"

"The root races."

"The what?"

"Well, the reason why we can't find any evidence of the existence of Atlantis is because we keep looking for the kinds of artifacts we would make. But we are the Fourth Root Race and the Atlanteans were the Third Root Race."

"Oh."

I spent months thinking that if I believed the information, especially on Atlantis, I must be crazy. I even asked my family doctor if I was crazy. She said no.

What had started out as the desire to do God's will had brought me to a place where the world as I knew it was falling down around me. I was supposed to write a book, but I didn't even want to *tell* anyone about all my experiences.

And then, in the middle of all my fears about my sanity, I had a visit from an other-worldly being.

14

A Message From Pan

Something woke me. I looked at the clock: 3:00 A.M. I lay down and tried to go back to sleep. However, a strange feeling filled the room as if an intruder lurked at the foot of my bed. In the wispy nighttime darkness, I sat up and looked beyond my feet to the end of the bed. There was no one there.

I fell back on the pillow and closed my eyes, drifting off to sleep. But there it was again. My eyes popped open, I sat up, and I looked hard all around the room. Nothing. I let out the breath I'd been holding and lay back down again.

I wondered if the visitor was my ex-husband whose spirit had come to me just before he died of cancer. Whatever it was, this presence felt much more powerful.

John, sleeping peacefully beside me, gave me the strength to deal with my mounting fear. I snuggled up close to him. But I couldn't sleep.

I had the strange impression that the visitor wore what appeared to be a deer mask and antlers. It looked like a disguise. I lay in the dark and tried to figure out what was going on. It felt like something or someone was trying to communicate with me.

My fear was becoming difficult to manage. It was only with restraint that I did not wake John. I forced myself to take a slow, deep breath and realized that although I felt power and, in reaction, fear, I did not feel evil.

I knew what the dark force felt like, from my encounter with Satan in the first life regression. This was different. I took another deep breath and felt myself relax somewhat. Whatever it was, the being was not fighting me or dragging me down as Satan had. In addition, despite its vibration of power, the visitor's attitude was also tinged with something that almost felt like sorrow.

My inner eye saw, at the foot of the bed, a being standing upright like a man, wearing a mask like a buck or stag. Why the disguise? Perhaps so I wouldn't be afraid. That was the clue that solved the mystery. I realized that my visitor was Pan, lord of the woodlands, wild animals, fields, and shepherds. No wonder he had to be in disguise. Pan is often depicted as having the furry legs, horns and ears of a goat. This image has also been used to portray the Devil.

Evidently the early Christian church wanted to frighten people away from the nature religions by making Satan in the image of Pan. However, I knew that Satan was a dark force, not a being with cloven hooves, horns, and a tail.

Moreover, according to mythological legend, it is Pan who plays his pipes so that nature works in harmony. For sure, if I had awakened to the church image of Satan standing at the foot of my bed, I would have screamed in terror. No wonder he was in disguise.

I had first heard of Pan from the Findhorn community in Scotland where humans work in cooperation with the elemental forces of nature to produce fantastic gardens. They had discovered that the natural world operated entirely under God's will, unlike humanity which has free will. One of their group, Ogilvie Crombie, called Roc, was communicating with and seeing nature spirits.

In *The Findhorn Garden* by the Findhorn Community, Roc says that Pan declares himself to be the servant of God. Pan also vows that he and his subjects, the nature kingdom, would willingly come to the aid of humanity, even though mankind continually abuses nature, if humanity would only believe in the power of the nature kingdom and ask the natural world to help mankind.

When I first read this I was filled with hope. We had but to ask Pan for help, and nature would clean the Earth for us.

As I lay in bed remembering what I knew of Pan, I was gratified to realize that the figure was no longer frightening to me. What would Pan want with me? I had no idea. But, like it or not, I would not get any more sleep until I found out.

And so, not wishing to disturb my husband's sleep, I grabbed my robe and sat in our bathroom writing what I was hearing from Pan.

This writing was so much easier than my own. It turned out that Pan was responding to a subconscious concern of mine. The previous night, before going to bed, John and I had watched one segment of a television series on ancient prophecies.

This program had deeply affected me because it addressed the upheavals alluded to in my hypnosis sessions. However, most of the predictions described on the program, whether they were given by psychics such as Nostradamus, Edgar Cayce, and Gordon-Michael Scallion, or the apparition of the Virgin Mary who spoke to the children of Fatima, or the Hopi Indian Nation, or even scientists predicting global warming, all painted a future that was very grim which included earthquakes, hurricanes, the end of the world as we know it, famines, people crying for water, New York and Los Angeles submerged under water, etc.

But I had just seen a future that looked golden. Although there would be difficulties, represented by the swirling morass of evil, it would just fall away, and the Golden Ones would survive to bring in a New Age. It was as if the earth changes were meant as an opportunity for cleansing and for bringing in a new life. Therefore, as I'd fallen asleep that night, I had wondered if I might actually have something to tell the world.

And so, when I finally got my pen and pad and took the time to listen to the thoughts coming from the antlered being, the first thing I heard was that just as we humans are feeling despondent as we come into these times of change, Pan, too, is in despair.

He is so discouraged because those who in their fear and greed may cause nuclear holocaust will also destroy the natural world, which is under Pan's dominion. The deer in the forest, the mouse in the field, the butterfly, the hummingbird, the flowers, the plants that create our food, the leaves that produce the oxygen we breathe, the rocks that purify our water, will also be destroyed. These are all of Pan's charges.

Furthermore, he did not like the wimpy, wishy-washy, namby-pamby way I had started the book. I should be more forceful.

The following is information as I heard it from Pan. This is how he felt I should start the book. (The "I" refers to me, Carole.):

"This book is written for the sincere ones. It is time for them to awaken.

"These are the people who, in Atlantis, were given or took upon themselves the task of preparing the Earth for a new Golden Age—the thousand years of peace on Earth. These, the Golden Ones, are here now, through reincarnation, ready and waiting to be awakened.

The time is now. Awaken!

"This is that time for which we prepared in Atlantis—again a time of heightened frequency of earth energy. The monument known today as the Great Pyramid was positioned so that it would be in exactly the correct alignment with the stars to be activated in the New Age.

"It is that time again to prepare a new race, this time the Fifth Root Race, for the new Earth is about to be born. We are in the throes of her labor.

"There are those among us who have the memory, since Atlantean times, of what to do. There are many people throughout the world who have the knowledge. It is my place to awaken them. I was given the task to know when the time had come.

"I am only the bell, the alarm clock, the reveille horn that says:

Awaken. Now is the time. The Earth needs you. This is the time that was foretold. This is the time that your life is about. Awake!

"This is what the earth cleansing is about. When it's all over, only the Golden Ones will remain.

"These predictions you hear of terrible apocalypses, Armageddon, the end of time, appear so terrifying. My message is of hope, but it is of a different type of hope. It is about the birth of a new world on the Earth.

"The hope is in the vision of the sincere people I saw—hundreds and thousands of them. They don't know what to do yet, but they will when the time is right. They are sincere about working with the Earth, with natural law, with universal law. Their motto is:

Above all, do no harm.

"I am also taking the time to write about reincarnation because many people will die. This is what most of the prophecies are about—the ways that people are going to die. But we are all—except those who go out the Star Gate with the Christ—going to die anyway. What's so new about that?

"The reality is that we have, most of us, died so many times before. And so many times we have become alive to a life after death—a life on the other side. And then we have been born again into another life here on Earth.

"Death and rebirth is a gift. If we had only one life to live, we would never have enough time to grow and change. That's why Christ said that only by being reborn could we receive everlasting life.

"This is a time of high intensity in the Earth. The Earth goes through these periods of self-purification. It is the nature of this planet to do so. The sun's earth and moon do a dance, periodically,

91

in which great geological changes occur on Earth. This is the time, This is also a time of opportunity for evolution—all of the natural world is affected."

Besides giving me advice on how to start the book, Pan also offered suggestions as to what all people can do:

"More people should garden. As much as possible, grow things, show an attempt to work with nature.

"Natural forces want to work with us but have been disappointed so many times. If nothing else, grow something just to see how difficult it is to grow, because then you can honor it even more. Fail. It doesn't matter. Just try. Every tree, plant, bird, rabbit, deer, and fish wants to know that we appreciate that they live, that they provide food for us, that they cleanse the air we breathe, that they fill our lives with joy and beauty."

"Begin now," Pan begs us. His world is dying because we are destroying the natural world—stupidly, because we, too, despite our fancy homes and buildings, were created in the natural world, for the natural world. We, too, need the wilderness, clean air, fresh water, trees, plants, and wild animals.

But remember, Pan has also said that nature can and wants to heal the Earth. We have only to appreciate how much nature does for us and ask for its help.

Pan said, "Work with us. Make gardens. Grow a plant. Like it. Eat it. Hunt animals for food. Honor our existence. Use us. Need us. We need you to preserve our homes. They don't have to be big, the changes you make. When you clear a subdivision, don't clear-cut. Leave trees, brush—homes for birds, rabbits, and raccoons. Make small changes in what you do.

"We, too, feel the upheavals that are coming.

"Carole is too much concerned that those of you who die may consider yourselves condemned. It is not so. It is the natural order of things. We in the natural world are well aware of this. We die that others may live. We decompose to nourish the soil.

"There is presently an opportunity for a natural ordering of things.

"One of the reasons why the sincere people must now begin to come forward, awaken, grow plants, love nature, is like the story in the Bible—*if ten good men can be found, God will save the city. Yes, except that in this case it is the Earth that will be saved. We want you to do it.* (The story about ten good men refers to the story of Sodom and Gomorra in the Old Testament. God assures Abraham that God will not destroy these wicked cities if, living within them, there are ten good men. However, there is only one good man, so God's angels take the man and his family out of the city, saving them from the destruction.)

"Hunt. I mean it. Hunt for food. Don't go into the woods like a drunken maniac. Hunt with reverence. Pray. Be thankful for the animal that has given its life that you may live. Throughout human history a true hunter is a truly holy person. It is difficult to kill a beautiful animal. Give thanks. A supermarket existence, in which children do not even know that potatoes push through the ground to grow, that milk comes from cows, that orange juice comes from trees, and that eggs come from chickens, is so far from any appreciation of the natural world.

"We want prayers for our dearly departed, reverence for lives given, appreciation for the good, and protection of our homes. We want acknowledgment that we create your oxygen and the materials that make your homes and furniture. We want you to daily remember that we create the life you so jealously hoard.

"We don't want you to continue to use and produce more and more man-made materials, because that totally destroys our wilderness. It pollutes the air, destroys the water—which the natural world as well as humanity needs to live. We want you to use the wilderness, to revere it—use it with reverence and thanksgiving.

"I know that many of you fear the wild places. But that is because you fear the wild places within yourself. You do not understand our way of life—the natural life. If you did, you would

93

not fear it or fear the wilderness within yourself. However, just in faith, knowing that wherever you live, the wild places are the sources of your oxygen and clean water, please revere us. Let us live and sustain you.

"Let each reverent person show themselves now. Pray over your food:

'The Earth has given this to me from its bosom that I may live. Praise be to every animal, every plant, every rock, insect and creeping thing that makes my world exist. Praise be to Allah. Amen. Praise to those who care for, capture, slaughter my food. Amen. The Earth sustains us. Praises.'"

(By the way, as far as I, Carole, am concerned, please feel free to substitute whatever makes you feel comfortable for "Allah"— God, Goddess, Yahweh, The Great Spirit, Buddha, Vishnu, Indra, The Force, the Universal Forces, The Creator, Life, Science, Hope—whatever brings to mind that which is greater than yourself.)

Pan says to the sincere people:
"On your knees, or with reverence, pray:

"What am I to do, God? Tell me what am I to do?

"Then measure what you hear against your common sense. And if what you hear, feel, intuit measures well against your common sense, do it. Say it. Love it. Give it."

He also suggests that we put our money where our mouths are, literally, since our food and life depend on the health of the wilderness. Donate money toward protecting the wilderness, toward saving protected park, and national forest lands.

In addition, he suggests to people with businesses that pollute, destroy habitats, etc.—anyone with power in this area—"Begin now to do whatever you can. Again, let your motto be: DO NO HARM, but if that is impossible immediately, at least DO <u>LESS</u> HARM. Ask for the intuition and the insights. They will come to you just as your business acumen comes to you in intuitive insights. You can do less harm and eventually no harm and still be successful. It will come to you. We and the Earth will feel it. We want to work with you."

For all, Pan says:
"Live as <u>naturally as possible. Get more sunlight</u>. Go outdoors at lunch break. Read outside. Allow little children who are imprisoned in schools to go outside when they work. Let them feel the sunlight, the breeze. Live more by daylight hours. <u>The natural light makes you and us stronger.</u>

"Say in how you live, '*I belong to the natural world.*' Depend on it and give thanks.
"To <u>those who will die, your time will come. You will be reborn into a new world. You will be reborn</u> as new people—the Fifth Root <u>Race.</u> You go to prepare in the afterlife. You will die to be spared your suffering. Death will release you. This is always the purpose of death. Be not afraid. Everyone has a place in the coming drama."

Pan says <u>that the essence</u> of the previous prayers is that in the new life, the new race of humanity will work *with* nature, even *Pan*. They will work *with* natural law, even *gravity*. They will work *with* universal law, even the *Creator*. Begin now.

And now Pan reminded me that I myself had already had an experience of how humanity and its interaction with the natural world was saved. Evidently it would do good to relate that story because it would show the kind of power people have who are sincere but who do not know they have the power to save things. So I am going to tell you the story of how the Toronto Island community was saved.

       *   *   *

When We Were Gods

I lived on Toronto Island during my twenties. It is an archipelago of islands in the huge bay that makes up Toronto Harbor. Most of the islands, although they were once inhabited, are now beautiful park land with restaurants, a petting farm, and a couple of yacht clubs. A ferry service takes passengers to three stops on the islands, including Wards Island where a community of about 800 lives.

Evidently the Toronto Island community is an amazing example of high-density population without the pollution, crime, and desocialization that normally accompanies such living arrangements. The houses are so close together that, should you have an animated discussion with a companion in your home during the summer when all the windows are open, you risk comment from your neighbors. In fact, your neighbor on your right may shout through your home to your neighbor on your left.

There are no cars on the Island, and the yards are small. Because we all traveled on the ferries to and from work, we all sat together at rush hours. It wasn't the kind of place where you could easily keep a secret. Nonetheless, the residents were not at each others' throats. On the contrary, there was an amazing sense of community.

Toronto Island was like heaven on Earth for me and for many of the other 800 residents living there because we lived surrounded by nature, yet only a 15-minute ferry ride from our jobs in Metropolitan Toronto.

However, the city owned the land on which our houses were built. We paid rent for the land. For various reasons, some of the people who made the major decisions at City Hall on the mainland had decided that people could no longer live on the Island. The city wanted to make the inhabited part of the Island into a manicured park like the rest of the Island.

Evidently there was a list detailing which houses would be demolished first. Many of us went and stood, hand in hand, in front of the bulldozers. I believe only one house was actually torn down.

A Message From Pan

We all went to the city chambers and sat on the benches while these strangers decided whether we had the right to live in our homes that were interspersed so beautifully with the natural surroundings. We all went, young and old, children and babies. We just sat there. Some of us acted as spokespeople for the group. The newspapers and television cameras were there. At the time, there were severe housing shortages in the city, and so it made no sense whatsoever to throw all 800 of us out of our homes. This was the first round, and we won it easily.

The Island had an occasional newspaper called *The Goose and Duck*, which kept us well informed of whatever was going on in the city chambers. It was the first place my photographs were published.

However, a couple of years later when there was no longer a housing shortage, the city tried again to demolish our houses by pointing out that because of our septic tanks, our houses were not up to building codes. Instead of simply updating the infrastructure of the Island, our septic tanks were going to be the reason to call in the bulldozers.

Fortunately there were lawyers among us who donated their time for our defense. During the ongoing legal battle, there were many times when bulldozers were evidently "on their way." I had meanwhile moved to Nova Scotia because my first husband had decided to attend college there. Nonetheless, I heard wonderful stories of how the Island was finally saved.

The Islanders really got into the spirit of things and established a home guard, a sort of militia without firearms. If I can remember correctly the stories I heard, with typical tongue-in-cheek enthusiasm each street appointed sergeants who wore football and construction helmets and whose duty it was to give the rallying orders for the residents of their small streets. I heard about drills in which people ran from their houses to meet in pre-designated boats, and from there they stormed in front of the pretend bulldozers. The people simply refused to be moved.

And they were not! A proper sewage system was installed. I believe they now have renewable 99-year leases on their land.

Their pretty little homes, nestled among poplars, with birds singing in the overhanging branches, remain. The bees continue to buzz in flowering vines climbing over the cottage windows. Every autumn the migrating monarch butterflies cluster on the trees, turning them orange. Every spring the Canada geese and mallards return to the lagoons as the Old Squaws and Buffleheads leave for their breeding grounds in the Canadian north.

Pan wanted to bring to my remembrance that people can and do live harmoniously with nature—even in the modern man-made world—rather than only in the Amazon rain forest where we would think it more likely.

Evidently Pan and the natural world were satisfied with the arrangement of people and nature on Toronto Island and still are. In addition, Pan wanted to remind me that ordinary, nature-loving people have, and can, peacefully, and quietly, without fanaticism or extremism, preserve and save areas where nature and people coexist to the benefit of both. The people merely have to be sincere and tireless in their determination.

Once the book was at the printer's office and nothing could be changed, I had the most phenomenal garden. My sunflowers were over 12 feet tall.

My peppers were the size of squashes. I can only assume that Pan and the other nature spirits were showing me how pleased they were to be included in the book and to show, in a small way, what the nature kingdom can do when they are appreciated.

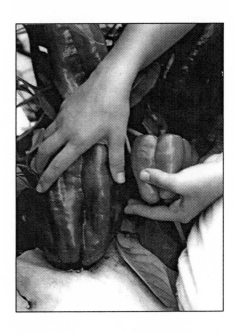

15

Flying Snake

And so, although I was inspired by my encounter with Pan, or whoever it was that I had "heard," I was now even *more* burdened with the feeling that I must be crazy. What *would* people say?

I spent a number of months filling my life with mundane comforting activities such as working on my beloved organic garden. Gardening was especially comforting because my deceased grandmother had interrupted one of my hypnosis sessions to tell me, in Ukrainian, that if I was so worried about my weight, why wasn't I taking better care of her mother's garlic.

Just before my 90-year-old grandmother died, she had handed me the garlic which her mother had given to her when she left the Old Country over 70 years ago. My grandmother had kept it going by faithfully replanting it all these years. Her mother had been the healer in the village, and this particular strain of garlic was supposed to be especially potent.

Three weeks before she had her final cardiac arrest, Baba ordered me to bring the garlic hanging in her garden shed to the hospital. She laid the braids of the dried roots on her hospital bed. Among them was an unusual plaiting, almost in the form of a half-wreath. She told me that just before her heart attack, three of her surviving Old Country girlfriends—old crones who used to occasionally visit Baba—had helped her to plait the braid at the end of the harvest. She handed this semi-circular braid to me and proclaimed that it would now be up to me to keep it going.

Then she asked me if I remembered everything she had taught me. It was then that I realized that my whole life she had been teaching me how to grow various foods and how to harvest, prepare, and preserve them. Although it appeared that most of what she taught me was about preparing food, I remembered that the different recipes were for different ailments. For example, chicken soup with celery was good for recovery from illness, but with parsley root, it would increase breast milk, etc.

I had felt honored that she would pass her mother's garlic on to me until I realized that I was the only granddaughter who had daughters. This knowledge was to be handed down through the females in the family.

Therefore, my garden was especially important to me, and even though I could only crawl along the rows that spring, I faithfully weeded the rows of garlic and planted onions and lettuce, as my grandmother had taught me.

For fertilizer we had purchased chickens that roosted in a little house John had built. The chicken droppings were used to nurture the soil. Clair, who loves all kinds of animals, was home from college many weekends helping to finish the chicken house and build the fence that would keep the poultry safe from marauding dogs and birds of prey.

Ah, motherhood!

One day I was transplanting tomato seedlings while Clair completed the final touches on the chicken run.

Suddenly, chickens began to squawk and ran for cover.

"Look, Mom, up above!" Clair shouted. Standing on a ladder, she stopped hammering bird netting to the roof of the chicken house and pointed up to the sky.

Flying Snake

In the distance a dark irregularly shaped spot grew as it approached. It was a hawk. Something that looked like a lion's tail hung from its talons. As it came closer, I could see it carried a snake. They passed directly overhead.

"Wow!" shouted Clair as she stepped from the ladder and pulled off her work gloves, striding to meet me. "You know something big is coming when the chickens run for cover."

I smiled, remembering the first time I had encountered the eagle and the snake. It had been on my bicycle trip, the morning of the day that I injured my ankle.

As Clair and I rested on lawn chairs in the shade, I said, "Clair, I just realized something about this strange stuff that's happened to me recently—you know, with my hypnosis sessions . . ."

One of her eyebrows went up in a question.

"Well," I went on, "it just occurred to me that it actually started years ago on my bicycle trip."

Clair gave me her famous stare, "OK, Mom, what are you talking about?"

"Well, the question I was asking then has finally been answered now."

"And the question ... ?"

"I guess it's the same one you're asking yourself: Who am I? What am I doing here? Where am I going?"

Clair sighed, "You got that one right." She looked at me, and I started my story.

With my feet up on a lawn chair, I reminisced out loud. "It was the summer after my first year studying photography and filmmaking. I was really confused. Somehow I thought that riding a bicycle through the Maritimes might help me see things more clearly.

"Right at the end of the trip—it took three weeks—I camped by a river. Just before dawn I awoke and stumbled toward the water. A heavy mist lay on the river. Suddenly, the fog burst into a wall of gold. The sun had broken through the horizon on the other side of the river.

"At the same time, to the right of me and hidden in the glowing mist, I heard a scuffling sound. There was something thudding and thumping to the right of my foot in the fog. It sounded like fighting.

"Before I could think or move, it was rising beside me. Ascending through the fog was a huge bird. Instinctively, I raised my arms to protect myself and also to block the blinding light from the sun rising over the layer of mist.

"The bird hung above me, its massive wings outstretched and grasping the thick morning air. Wispy sunlight poured around the long, extended wingtip feathers.

"In that instant, with the bird's body blocking the sun, I saw the white head and the white tail. It was a bald eagle. Our eyes met. The eagle's golden eyes were wild. They spoke to me of power and freedom.

"As the eagle rose out of the mist, I saw captive in the gnarled talons, a snake. Still alive, the reptile flicked out its tongue at me. The eagle's massive black wings pumped over my head. As it rose, the snake passed before my eyes. I gasped.

"No kidding," said Clair.

"No kidding," I replied. "The eagle lifted the snake over the mist, over the rising sun, and over the treetops.

"That image has remained emblazoned upon my mind throughout my life. It looked like the silhouette of a snake flying with big black wings.

"I watched them until my heart slowed its furious beating, and I could no longer see them.

"But, I had no idea what it meant. I only knew that it was powerful and it had stirred me to the depths of my being. I also felt as if, somewhere deep within me, something had been answered. It felt as if a compass had been set and now I was pointed in the right direction."

I looked over at Clair.

"You never figured out what it meant?" she said.

"No," I replied.

"I think I read somewhere," Clair said, "that the Native Americans say the eagle is supposed to be a messenger of the gods."

I shrugged, "But what would the gods want with a snake?"

I shifted so I looked out at the garden glistening in the sunlight and buzzing with bees. "You know what, Clair?" I said, turning to her slowly, "I just remembered. A couple of days before I saw the eagle and snake, something *did* happen that told me who I was."

Clair looked at me quizzically and stretched out her long lanky legs as if she was ready to keep listening.

"That was the night I camped at a truly beautiful campground. My tent site was on a long spit of land surrounded on three sides by water. It was wonderful—with a wrap-around view of the sky.

"There was a gorgeous sunset. Then the sky darkened as one by one the stars came out. I stayed by my fire while it burned down to embers enjoying the beautiful view. When it was dark, I crawled into my tent and fell instantly to sleep.

"In the middle of the night, I awoke because I had to go to the bathroom. The restroom was way at the other end of the spit of land in the main part of the campground in a stand of trees.

"Half-asleep, I crawled out of my tent. However, before I was fully standing, I saw a terrifying sight. The sky was moving. It had become unhinged. A huge chunk of the night sky billowed over the water and floated upward. It shimmered red, then turned to green. To the right, a large golden spot pulsated to the sound of a drum.

"Half asleep, I felt confused and frightened. What was happening? The sky was coming apart as if it was made of puzzle pieces. The world must be ending. Without thinking, I fell on both knees and elbows. My head dropped to the ground. I cupped my hands over my mouth and made hooting sounds, like an owl, into the earth.

"It was as if I was calling into the earth for help. I was totally on automatic.

"But, the sky did not come crashing down. After awhile, my conscious mind began to awaken. I began to realize the strange things I was doing, on my elbows and knees, hooting into the earth. I hoped no one else was awake and watching me.

"Although I was beginning to think, I still had no idea what was wrong with the sky.

"But, I still had to go to the bathroom. Like it or not, I would somehow have to get to the bathroom under that terrifying expanse of sky.

"Holding my hands like blinders on a horse, I kept my eyes on the pine-needle path under my feet. Stooped over, I ran to a stand of trees at the edge of the spit of land.

"There, surrounded by the trees, I felt protected and safe, like a little animal hiding in the bushes. With my hands covering my eyes, I slowly straightened up. I moved first one finger and then another until I could see the sky through my fingers.

"There was no doubt about it. The sky was really moving. It billowed and heaved like a gigantic curtain, extending from horizon to horizon."

"Northern Lights!" said Clair, triumphantly.

I smiled. "You got it, you're right. But, when I'd been half-asleep, my mind had been asleep too. I'd never seen the Aurora before except on television. It was so much larger billowing above me, than on a tiny screen. And, it seemed to be alive, not like the dead little image flickering in my living room.

"The next morning, when I stopped for breakfast, people were talking about it. There was evidently a newspaper article—unusual sunspot activity for that time of year—and a much greater display than had ever been seen in that area."

Clair shook her head, "but the weird thing was what you were doing, 'whoo, whoo, whoo.'"

"No kidding. That's when I discovered something about who I was.

I realized that I was much more than what I appeared to be. The "I" that was me was *both* a conscious being and *also* an unconscious being.

"When I left on my quest, I had thought that by asking the question: 'Who am I?' I was looking for my career or the direction of my life.

To my surprise, I had received an answer to the much greater question: 'Who am I really?'

"Now I knew that there was this whole other world within me— or anyway, that I was connected with this whole other world that I normally was totally unconscious of. My experience showed me that the unconscious was a real thing and that there was nothing to fear from it. It was obviously deeply concerned with my survival.

"A couple of mornings later, I was startled by the eagle and the snake.

Clair picked up a four-leafed clover from the grass at our feet. "What I'd like to know," she said, "is why do all the adventures happen to you?"

"Come on, Clair," I said as I stood up and stretched. "Your life has just begun. If my hypnosis sessions are even half-way right, you may have a really great adventure ahead of you."

16

The Fifth Root Race

I encountered the Northern Lights and flying snake during the first two weeks of August, 1972. Interestingly, Bob Frissell, in his unusual book, *Nothing in this Book Is True, But It's Exactly How Things Are*, says that on August 7, 1972, our sun experienced the most severe storm ever recorded. He goes on to make the controversial claim that if aliens from Sirius had not stepped in, everything on Earth would have been killed. Maybe the dramatic event I saw that night really was a potential end of the world. It certainly felt like it. In any case, it jolted my unconscious awake.

Frissell's book is also intriguing because he says that aliens are intervening so that there will be no cyclical earth changes this time around. Instead, he claims we will all have the opportunity to transcend the physical and ascend. Perhaps my information is based on what my soul knew in Atlantis and doesn't include these new developments. I hope so.

Meanwhile, I continued to care for the garlic and chickens. Although this was healthy and comforting, it was not getting the book written.

After about four months of puttering around, I began to itch all over. The doctor thought it was a contact allergy and suggested a salve that worked only temporarily. I started to itch all over again.

When I finally figured out that I was being reminded to get back to my computer, the itching went away. As I wrote a little, I found I could write more. However, I still feared that if I believed the information, I might be crazy. Therefore, I decided that I would write it without believing it.

To keep myself going, I fueled my resolve with fantasies of the money I might make and the fame I might have once the book was published. I saw myself on the Oprah Winfrey Show, agonized over being intimidated by David Letterman, and worried about how fat I'd look on camera.

Now I had a new problem. What was the best way to write the book so it would be sensationally popular? I must have rewritten the chapter on Atlantis at least five times. Throughout that summer and into the autumn, I rethought my original outline over and over again. But no matter how hard I tried, I couldn't get it right. The more I wrote, the more questions I had. I believed that I couldn't proceed because I didn't know enough.

I called Lynn for another appointment, bringing with me a six-page sheaf of questions. After I was hypnotized, I found myself again on the summit of the white mountain at the top of the world. Again I saw the three wise men. As before, they were clothed in loose robes. Whereas before their heads had been uncovered, they were now covered with hoods so that I could barely see their faces. They stood silently before me.

The first time I had seen them, they had looked out over the world. This time they looked at me. I climbed the last few feet of the summit to the cave at the top, again entering through an opening on the right side of the cave.

Inside the cavern I floated before the hooded savants in the same position that I reclined in the easy chair in Lynn's office. The Christ stood beside me holding my right elbow, His loving kindness pouring out to me as before. Mary, the Holy Mother, stood on my left, my left hand in hers. Occasionally she would pat my hand as if to give me strength. I felt immense love from both the Christ and Mary.

The three wise men, however, were quiet, hushed, contemplative and not especially warm. They felt neutral but definitely involved and intent on what was going on.

Lynn made the suggestion that I should experience whatever I could even if it surprised me. There had been so many times in previous sessions when my conscious mind had cried, laughed, or fought against the outlandish scenes I saw.

First Lynn asked me some of the questions on my prepared list.

"Are you right in assuming that the experiences you have had in the lives given were representative of the first four root races?"

I saw the word and answered, "Yes."

So now I knew that I had been shown these unusual lifetimes because it was a foundation for the history of the soul on Earth.

Lynn listed the four root races:

First: Light beam.
Second: Wisp-of-smoke, translucent amber being.
Third: Going in and out of bodies in Atlantis.
Fourth and present root race: Modified animal bodies.

I answered "Yes" to all except the third or the Atlantean lifetime, in which I said, "Only partly." There would be more on the Third Root Race.

Then Lynn asked me what we should expect the Fifth Root Race to be like.

I said that they would be the babies of the Golden Ones. Apparently one of the purposes of this book is to alert the Golden Ones to the differences to expect in their children.

"I see the babies as golden," I said as I saw a mother holding a new baby. Its little arms reached up for its mother. The baby's skin was more golden, and it also glowed with a golden aura. It was a big, round-headed baby. The eyes were bulging, with puffy pockets under them. I could see the head, arms, and torso. The legs might have been smaller, vestigial, translucent, or invisible.

The babies "are a golden aura'd people. When they're born, they'll hold that aura, unlike us, who sink into murky colors. They hold the aura in that clear, bright Light. They have the ability to be that aligned."

The colored light bands surrounding a person, visible only to a few people, are called the aura. The halo around the Virgin Mary and Christ are artists' renditions of the aura. Recently a procedure known as Kirlian photography has been invented, which can photograph the aura.

As an example to myself, while hypnotized, I began to feel in my solar plexus how I muddled the colors of my own aura. I felt the fatigue caused by my resentments, the numbness caused by my fears, and the tension caused by my need to have things go my way. These negative emotions, based on a lack of faith in good, muddied my aura so that its colors were no longer bright and clear.

The Fifth Root Race will be very different from us in that they won't even know how to have these negative emotions. They will *always* have hope, faith, and love. Their aura colors will always remain clear. "They're different," I said. "They're very loving people. They do no harm."

As I watched the mother with her glowing infant, I was shocked by what I saw next. However, I remembered Lynn's suggestion at the beginning of the session to allow myself to be surprised.

I saw the child disappear in the mother's arms. When it was gone, the mother's face contorted in fear and shock. "I see that it's rejuvenation," I continued. "They won't age like we do."

So this was how they would triumph over death. They could rejuvenate themselves because their bodies were not as tightly bound in the physical as we are. They could change the characteristics of their physical nature—moving from solid to Light body easily. We had less ability to rejuvenate because our bodies were so comparatively dense.

I saw the baby come back into the physical so it could be seen again. It laughed at its mother, who had been concerned because it had disappeared. "They'll be like Casper the Ghost," I said.

"They'll do things that will be really strange," I continued, and then I sighed. "They really need to be loved. They will come only to people who love."

Then I added, "Oh yes. And the Fifth Root Race will not be born until this, what we call 'evil,' has passed—[until] this generation [has passed]—which means that the Golden Ones will survive. They will endure because they are meant to bring in this Fifth Root Race."

Next I was told that a recent dream I had had about the survivors of the upheavals was true. In the dream, I had found a pile of dead, bloodied people who looked as if they had been battered by powerful forces such as volcanic earthquakes and then piled by gigantic tidal waves.

Among them was a naked, skinny boy who was still alive and covered in blood. He was so cold. I got clothes for him to wear to protect and warm him. There were others, about a half dozen in this one place, all young people. I hoped I would have enough clothes to keep all of them warm. They looked stunned and shocked by the tragedies they had lived through.

That same night I had also dreamt about a number of children I found hidden in a cave. They were sleeping deep under the earth in the sand along the seashore. They hid in the cave for protection until the earth upheavals were over. I came by and told them it was time to wake up and come out now. Everything was safe again.

"And so there will be upheavals?" asked Lynn.

"Oh, yes," I answered with great sadness.

When Lynn asked me when we should expect the first earth changes, I replied in August 1997. I saw a map of Australia and explained that the first shifting would be just off the Northwest coast of Australia. I saw it off the bump in the curve between the north and west, what I've learned is the Kimberley Peninsula and Derby area.

The movement would be only the first creak of tension. Over time, the shudders would mount until eventually the Earth's crust would slide over the core.

The first earth movements would be almost imperceptible, similar to the way a top first wobbles very slightly before the wobbling becomes more and more pronounced and the top finally falls. The August 1997 quake would merely be the first quiver—not even a wobble, almost like a slightly ragged breath.

This session was held on October 31, 1996. A list of earthquakes at the Internet address http://geology.usgs.gov/eq/archive confirmed an earthquake on August 10, 1997, at 16.52 S and 123.58 E, which is exactly off the bump in the curve in the Northwest of Australia—exactly where I saw it during the hypnosis. Just as it took me a year to find the courage to approach the man of my dreams, I didn't look up the earthquake until a year after I'd predicted it would happen.

I began to do research on earth changes. In *Fingerprints of the Gods*, Graham Hancock describes an intriguing theory that Antarctica is actually Atlantis, moved to the South Pole by a gigantic displacement of the Earth's crust sometime before 4,000 B. C. when Antarctica was not yet covered by a mile-thick ice sheet. The idea is that the ice sheet grew once the land mass on which Atlantis rested was moved to the South Pole.

This theory also explains the Ice Age. The lands that were suddenly covered with ice were moved from temperate locations to extreme northern locations because of the earth upheavals.

When the Earth's crust moved again, the lands in the North were relocated to more temperate areas of the globe and the ice melted. This theory could explain why North America and Europe were alternately in temperate areas, and then covered by ice. Whenever they were moved into northern latitudes, they were suddenly covered in ice. When moved to temperate latitudes, the ice melted.

Albert Einstein sanctified the possibility of such a monumental crustal displacement in his foreword to Charles H. Hapgood's 1953 book, *The Earth's Shifting Crust*. Einstein wrote that the spin of the Earth acts on the great mass of the ice fields at the poles, which creates a centrifugal potential that could eventually cause the

Earth's crust to shift over the inner part of the Earth like an orange skin shifting over the flesh part of an orange.

I've also read Immanuel Velikovsky's *Worlds in Collision*, in which he theorizes that the Earth's crust has previously undergone massive displacements when the planet was hit by a huge comet.

Despite these theories and the fact that I correctly predicted the Australian earthquake, I don't personally believe that there will be gigantic earth upheavals. I think that likely the upheavals I saw were indications of upheavals within myself. For example, the opening of a spiritual center or even uncovering traumatic childhood memories. However, in trance I saw it differently.

"And so the changes will be geological?" asked Lynn.

"Yes," I replied. "The fear within the natural world and with all of us in the Brotherhood [whatever that's about] is that all of us are feeling this [the imminence of these earth changes] now. All the animals, everything on Earth—and some of the people—go nuts.

"And they [the ones who go nuts] are experiencing it as greed," I added. "They want to hoard as much as they can for fear that they'll have nothing—meaning money, people, power—whatever in the past made them think that they were getting love.

"But they don't get love that way. So the fear is that these people will and are about to destroy the Earth and all of humanity."

I said that the best way to prepare for the possibility of earth changes was to love. "There's no better preparation than to love. Love those who despicably use you. Pray to the angels, or your Guides, or Christ—whoever you believe in—to help you to love, for your own sake." Then I repeated more quietly and with depth, "For your own sake."

Evidently, although I consciously thought that the best way to prepare for natural disasters of such magnitude would be to store food, have a non-electric water source, and live in safety lands, my superconscious mind, which was concerned with our everlasting souls, felt that there was no better preparation than to love.

If we loved, we would have our priorities straight. That way, if we were among those destined to die in the upheavals, we would die with love in our hearts, at peace with ourselves. If we lived, we would need to love and cooperate with other survivors to get us through the difficult times. If we could love, it would also be easier for our spiritual guides to work with us.

"Has it already been set who will live and who will not?" asked Lynn.

"There is, yes, a group that have been awaiting their destiny at this time, that are part of us, that have the key to open the time of peace." These are the Golden Ones.

17

The Brotherhood

Next we wanted to get some answers about the troubling chapter on Atlantis. Lynn asked me why I had felt so blocked. The answer was that I feared the information would be misused because of the technical nature of the Unified Field Theory, the scientific basis of the Crystal power.

Then I felt myself really being scrutinized by the men in the hoods. They were stern, still, and very serious. I floated in front of them, my body reclining in space. Behind them was the stone wall of the mountain. The stone floor stretched between us. Above us was the high-vaulted ceiling.

Until this moment the session had flowed smoothly and easily. Now everything stopped. I waited. I became aware of the Christ standing by my right elbow, His protection and caring surrounding me. Mary, on my other side, held my left hand tightly in both her hands. I felt as if I was holding my breath.

Something was wrong.

I realized that I was on trial and had been found wanting by the Brotherhood. (For some unknown reason I kept calling these men in hoods "The Brotherhood.") Although I could not see their faces because of the shadows cast by their hoods, I knew they were staring at me. No words passed between us, but I understood what they told me. They showed me how I had been fantasizing about becoming famous, imagining that the book would become wildly popular. Of course they were absolutely right about my thoughts.

They were being especially stern with me now. I was almost in tears. "Because I messed up with the fame stuff. That's dangerous. And the skin condition and the itching is to frighten me."

The Brotherhood telepathically showed me how my need for fame could jeopardize everything. They said that I was part of the problem. This was one of the main reasons for my writer's block. They were holding me back from proceeding.

It made no sense to them how I could possibly spend so much time and energy on something that was so transitory. They showed me lifetime after lifetime in which I'd been first one kind of a person and then another. I was reminded of how, in the past life regressions on overweight, I'd been an American in the Old South, an African in a thatched hut, and an aristocrat in France.

Then they showed me how various vivid dreams I'd had throughout my life were also memories of past lives—a gypsy whose husband and child were killed, the fourth wife of a Plains Indian medicine man, a Japanese woman of leisure married to a powerful lord, a Mayan priest, and a gay sailor who plied the seven seas on square riggers with his lover.

The members of the Brotherhood showed me how, in previous lifetimes, I had had wealth, position, power, and beauty. I had lost all these qualities at the end of whatever lifetime I had had them in. And the wealth, position, power and beauty had never really made me happy because there was no peace in them. These qualities were absolutely fleeting compared to the enormity of my reality as an eternal Light Being.

Next followed a telepathic discourse between myself and the members of the Brotherhood. First I was reminded that my deepest soul purpose was to help humanity.

Telepathically I answered that to help humanity seemed so confining and boring compared to being beautiful.

Communicating without words, they conveyed to the Christ standing beside me, "That's where *her* greatest joy will come. Just as all the greedy people who want money and power—her greed is in fame. She thinks that fame will give her love. But her real happiness comes from helping humanity."

It felt as though we were having a tug of war. I mentally replied, showing them how perfecting myself was a valid goal. Mary, standing on my left side, patted my hand sympathetically.

They agreed. But it wasn't enough. And it wasn't the whole story because the perfection of myself included living for others. In other words, my real self, my soul, which resonated with the spirit of the Creator, was deeply concerned with helping humanity.

They insisted that my greatest joy would come from aligning with my real self and helping others.

They showed me how even if I was the most beautiful woman on Earth, I would still not derive the same joy that I would from helping humanity. Instantly they showed me times in my life when I was slender and beautiful, and they compared my feelings at that time with instances when I had reached out to someone.

The times when I was "on the top" were also mingled with fears of being toppled. On the other hand, the helping occasions usually weren't great events, but they warmed me with an inner glow that even today makes me smile.

They reminded me of the many times when I hadn't even known that I had helped someone, and they showed me how good I had felt when I found out how much happier the person was— even when the person gave me no credit.

As I comprehended and accepted what they said, I saw the stern men in hoods adopt softer, almost smiling expressions on their mouths, which I could see below the hoods.

It made me sad to think that I'd been wasting so much of my life chasing a shadow. "The guys are lightening up," I said to Lynn. I could feel my breathing begin to normalize.

I realized that my greatest happiness would come from helping humanity, not because the Bible said so, but because it was what my soul was about. It was my real self. When I physically lived in alignment with my real self, I would resonate with joy.

Once I acknowledged this, I saw the faces under the hoods soften. "They're smiling now," I said.

Lynn continued reading out loud the many questions I had brought. One was about a secret chamber in or around the Great Pyramid. I'd had a dream—exactly the same dream *twice* in the same night, supposedly so I would remember every detail—in which I'd been told that I knew how to open this secret chamber that contained records from Atlantis. I wondered if there was more information on the location of this secret room and its contents. The stern ones became especially tense about this question. Then I heard and saw the answer, "No."

Immediately the Christ stood forward. The Brotherhood turned to Him. He began to interact with the hooded men, acting on my behalf as an advocate, defending me and challenging their decision. I didn't hear words because they were masked from me. After a while the Christ turned to me.

He began to tell me the result of His conference with the Brotherhood. It turned out that two of the hooded figures were the archangels Gabriel and Michael. The third was the Christ, Who assumed both His omnipotent role in the hooded robe and at the same time stood at my side as my friend.

They had conditions for me.

They began to show me details of a dream I had had years ago while married to my first husband, in which I'd been an Atlantean scientist. It was one of the reasons why I'd feared confronting my experiences in Atlantis.

The dream had started by showing me that it was about a different time from our own and so therefore the imagery would be translated into our present images. Then I'd seen myself tall and slender, with waist-length black hair, in a long black body-hugging shift, standing by a bar. The bartender had just put another drink down on the counter in front of me.

A man had approached me. He was dressed in Roman-style armor with a breastplate and teal colored feathers from the metal head guard that extended from his helmet down the sides of his face over the sideburn area. My breath had quickened as he touched my arm and then cupped his body behind mine in a sexual embrace. Whispering in my ear, he told me that he knew how weak I was and that I couldn't possibly resist him. Evidently this "Atlantean tank commander" had been my first husband in this lifetime.

My body told me he was right—I couldn't resist his seduction. I didn't care anymore. I knew I'd give in eventually. It might as well be now. He wasn't the first, and he wouldn't be the last.

He told me how much superior he was to me because he was a hard-bodied soldier—a man of discipline. I sighed and pressed myself against his body, the passion rising in me. He was right. I wasn't disciplined. I was needy and weak. But on the other hand, he was just a soldier, and I was a scientist. Without my know-how, the Crystal could not work. I had a great responsibility on my shoulders. It didn't really matter what I did because I was so superior to him that I could do whatever I wanted to. And anyway, I didn't see what harm it would do to lie with him.

And so I took him to my bed. And again. And again. After awhile he was my regular lover. Despite his derision of me, I had to admit that I was lonely and needed him. But I never had any illusions that he was just a simple soldier while I was an important, brilliant scientist. Because of my loneliness, sometimes I would answer his questions about the Crystal. It flattered me to see how impressed he was with information that I knew he had no way of understanding. He was one of the clones that had been developed to perform Atlantean military maneuvers.

One morning, after our coupling, we stood in the doorway of the Tower that held the Crystal, where I both worked and lived. In the distance I could see undulating green hills and a ziggurat-type tower, one of the reinforcement towers for the Crystal technology. But something was wrong. The distant tower shook and tilted.

I saw the earth that supported the tower rise up like a mountain and then crash down into a valley. The ground continued to move, heaving up into the air and then falling.

Suddenly I realized that I was watching the approach of a gigantic earth displacement advancing toward us in waves.

My mouth opened in terror as I looked to my companion. To my surprise, he was gloating. He laughed, the fool. Then I realized what had happened. Although he was incapable of understanding the Crystal technology, he had conveyed the words to his commander, Belial, who could understand the science. Using this information, Belial had tuned the Crystal too high. According to the Cayce readings, the Crystal was tuned too high to destroy marauding beasts that were terrorizing the people of Atlantis. There is speculation that these beasts could have been dinosaurs or mastodons.

According to the Cayce readings, Belial was the leader of the Sons of Belial who warred with the group called the Law of One. Absolutely and ruthlessly ambitious, Belial's whole purpose was self-aggrandizement at the expense of anything and anyone. He would stop at nothing to achieve his aims.

The problem was that the Crystal technology was never meant to be used for anything but good—no matter what the threat. By tuning it too high, the land, which was poised to shift because of the upcoming cyclical earth upheavals, could not handle the tightened vibrations and so began to erupt and crumble more violently than it would have from only natural causes.

When I awoke from the dream, I was mortified that because of my weakness I might have been responsible for the death of so many innocent people. However, I assumed that the dream was merely a nightmare. Now in the hypnosis session the archangels were telling me that the dream had been true. Not only had my carelessness led to the loss of so many lives, but also I had compromised the integrity of the Law of One in their struggle with Belial.

The stern men in the hooded robes said that my present life assignment, to awaken the Golden Ones, was partially to atone for my mistakes in Atlantis.

Immediately the archangels huddled with the Christ. When they opened up to me again, they telepathically told me to continue writing, indicating that they would keep watch and see if I'd be faithful this time—faithful to my purpose rather than, as in Atlantis, I had been faithful to my own ends. They suggested that I *might* be able to serve in Egypt, too, in the future. But certainly not in the frame of mind where they found me now. I would have to ask again once I finished the book.

As I hovered in the air in front of the hooded men, I was sure I could never write the book. There was no way I was going to reveal something that I'd rather keep a deep dark secret forever. It was like formulating the Theory of Relativity and then having to live with Hiroshima and Nagasaki for eternity. I didn't want anyone to know about my mistakes in Atlantis. My only redeeming hope was that no one would believe the story. It was the ultimate in craziness. And that was the absolute reason why I could not possibly write about it.

Telepathically I heard from the Brotherhood: "You are not going to get a beautiful body until you are faithful to your purpose."

There you have it. It was over. I likely would not be slender ever again.

"And it will be a gift to you. You can't make it happen because it's the one thing you want. And we've got leverage."

Next, I heard that the Second Coming was also a gift. I had to admit that I'd become secretly proud that I was one of the "chosen ones." Now I knew that the Second Coming was simply a potential for all of us.

I saw that the Second Coming operated under the same paradoxical rules of everything having to do with the spiritual world: it's not something that you go after and get, like you do in the physical. You can't attend the right church, meditate the right way, eat right, do the right charitable acts, have the proper past life regression. It's something that you let go of, and then it's given. In other words, it was grace.

Finally I heard, "This is a session of admonishment, just in case Carole didn't get it." Afterward I looked up "admonish" in John's old college *New Webster's Dictionary*. It said: "1. To warn, caution against specific faults; 2. To reprove mildly; 3. To advise, exhort; 4. To inform or remind, by way of a warning." I thought that just about said it all!

The Brotherhood also told me that I should first finish the book and then come for another session in which more would be given. Christ bent over and gave me a big hug. It was as if I'd been tried and found wanting, but He had been my advocate and defended me. I had another chance.

After Lynn brought me out of the hypnotic trance, I said to her, "I tell you, Lynn, Christ is my friend. There's these other elements—the men in the hooded robes, the archangels. It's not that they're mean—they're just sterner. Christ is truly our friend. He came here as our advocate. He likes us. Whereas these other Power Beings, they're not so sure. That's why Gabriel sounds the way he does. [He] just can't believe it. Like, 'What a mess [we've gotten ourselves into].'"

It occurred to me that Christ is our advocate and so kind to us because He, like us, has been imprisoned in the physical in various incarnations, including the one as Jesus. Therefore He knows how very difficult it is for us, how we cling to life, not knowing there is anything else beyond. He's been through it, and He knows just how hard it is, here on Earth, to follow God's will.

The archangels, on the other hand, have never experienced life on Earth in a physical form. Therefore, they don't and can't understand why we have so much antagonism to our lessons (suffering) and why we spend so much time accumulating, fighting for, and conniving for all the things on Earth that we think will make us happy, such as money, power, fame, glamour, and possessions.

To them it is so obviously futile, since our conscious living times on Earth are so short compared to the real life that we are in touch with when we sleep and when we are between lifetimes. This is why they have so little patience with us.

They also appear to be so stern because they have never and will never experience emotion as we know it. They have never been in modified animal bodies, and so they don't know grief, loss, desire. It isn't that they don't feel, but their feeling isn't associated with chemical changes such as a rush of adrenaline, secretions of hormones, or sympathetic nerve reactions to memories, etc.

I realized that since they have never been in physical bodies, their true form is probably pure Light. However, I saw them as men in hooded robes because my brain interprets everything in terms of itself, a human body. In addition, just as there is a Christ Consciousness, which is available to us at all times, there must also be a Gabriel and Michael consciousness that anyone can tap into. In later hypnosis sessions I did see them as immense beings of Light.

They did smile when I started to understand what they were telling me. They certainly do not understand my obsession with my body—something, from their point of view, that I have for such a short time, that is subject to the laws of aging and gravity, that I will soon cast off—except from the desire to align the physical with the eternal.

At first it was upsetting to hear that I'd never be thin again—or anyway, no chance of it until I'd finished the book as an expression of my desire to help humanity—very unlikely, if you asked me.

However, after awhile this revelation became very freeing. Now, for the first time since I was eleven years old and originally began to gain weight, I'm no longer mentally measuring the calories of every mouthful of food as I eat. It doesn't matter any more. I'm going to be fat no matter what. When I go for a walk, I'm no longer burning calories or revving up my metabolism, I'm just enjoying the outdoors and taking the dogs for a walk.

Paradoxically, I now have what I always wanted. I'm free of the preoccupation to make myself slender.

18

The Tower and the Crystal

You would think that after being told that I would have to tell the story of my part in the fall of Atlantis, I would have just shelved the whole writing project. But, I still wanted to be thin.

I decided to continue. However, the next time I entered Lynn's office, I was full of dread. Lynn and I had put off delving into my Atlantean life for almost a month, but I felt as though I had put of Atlantis for most of my adult life. It was time to truly confront it. What would I find?

This session had a pinkish-mauve color. Whenever I'd look for a lifetime in a past life regression, I'd see something that looked like a file drawer among an endless wall of file drawers. I assumed the file drawers represented all the entities connected with the Earth. I'd float to one. It would be mine. It would open. In it I'd see different colors of tissue paper arranged like files. They would represent my different lifetimes. They are mainly blues, pinks, mauves, and purples. The tissues would ruffle as if a breeze rippled through the colored papers. Then my attention would stop on one, the lifetime we'd be looking for. In this case it was a pinkish-mauve color.

Then I would usually see only black, and out of that would begin either a feeling or some other sense impression, often something I would see—in this case, a spider.

The spider stood motionless in a round room, its long black legs and white body forming a high inner dome within a chamber. It stood in the middle of a room surrounded by windows. The domed ceiling above the spider reminded me of our present-day optical telescopes used for observing stars.

Today, because we use machines such as telescopes and computers to accomplish work, we assume that machines would have been used in Atlantis as well. However, I was soon to discover that our lives in Atlantis were very different from what they are today.

As I examined the scene, there was no doubt that an actual spider had some kind of important function in this domed Atlantean tower—a large white-segmented spider with long black legs. And it was huge, almost filling the room, or else the room was as small as a spider!

In the center of the room, directly below the body of the spider and in the middle of the circular floor, crouched a green frog-like being on a platform. Dark hair covered his (or her) wide head, falling over his forehead. His wide-set, almond-shaped eyes flitted about and then stared as he concentrated. Long frog legs buckled and stretched as the little being swayed with the intensity of his work.

As I tried to comprehend the scene before me, I began to have the feeling I was not quite the same kind of person I am today. In fact, I *was* the pixie-like frog-being. I also noticed that everything in the circular chamber shone with a deep blue light.

I waited, allowing the full meaning of the scene to surface. There was a sense of having to control something. This something was powerful, and it was the frog being's function to direct it.

And then the full impact of what I was viewing hit me. It was the Crystal. The spider was being used as we would use a machine today—to hold and suspend the great and powerful Crystal that produced the power in Atlantis!

My conscious mind's ability to comprehend this strange scene was being stretched to its limits. And then:

The Tower and the Crystal

"My God, my right hand is somehow moving!" I said.

The fingers of my right hand twitched on the arm of the recliner where I lay in Lynn's office. In the past life memory, the hand was the padded-fingered hand of the frog-being. It moved an egg-shaped ball that floated in indigo light. The light contained in a white basin which looked like our present-day baptismal font, except that the whole appliance—a white basin containing blue light supporting the egg-shaped ball—floated in air.

The small end of the ball pointed straight up at the Crystal, held in the body of the spider. The large end of the ball floated in the blue light held in the floating basin.

There was a gold stripe around the bottom of the egg-shaped ball and a corresponding gold stripe along the rim of the white basin. The relationship between the gold stripes controlled the Crystal.

"It [the Crystal] is collecting electromagnetic waves," I said. "And repatterning them out of their random motion into orderly motion." I saw a grid. "And I know how to manipulate that so that it's at different frequencies."

There were many power stations, reminding me of the way radio waves from radio and television stations are transmitted today. I saw other white towers on hilltops against a background of forest. They were situated in a particular grid pattern. Evidently the towers locked the electromagnetic waves into a grid, making a type of power similar to magnets repelling themselves.

"These places are best constructed on a hill," I said, "but they're unlike our metal radio towers. It's more a ceramic of some sort. It's not even stone. I believe it's been forged in some way. The windows are part of how it works."

It was different from the way we make a power source today. In the 21st century, we build a tower that *holds* the equipment. However, in Atlantis, *all* the components of the tower operated together to produce the power.

When the energy flowed smoothly out from the tower, the white walls of the tall domed building vibrated. This resonant vibration, coupled with the triangular window-like openings at the top of the tower, beamed the re-patterned energy out in varying frequencies to the whole of Atlantis.

It was a type of energy that did not require a wire for transmission like our present-day electricity. Permeating everything, it was the energy of life itself. Similar to our radio and television waves, this field was and still is everywhere but invisible. We live in it—and it lives in and through us. It is partially ordered by large celestial bodies such as the sun, moon, and Earth through the force known as gravity. The field included gravitational waves as well as electromagnetic waves.

"It's the Unified Field Theory," I said. I saw it printed out in my mind's eye. I knew that in the 20th century, Albert Einstein had struggled unsuccessfully with the Unified Field Theory until his death. It still has not been solved today. However, in my Atlantean incarnation, I was seeing that the problem with integrating electromagnetic and gravitational waves was that the gravitational waves had a swell to them, similar to the ocean's large swells underneath the smaller surface waves.

To still the swell that distorted the gravity waves, three main towers were built in the troughs of the gravity waves. The position of the three main towers had to be exact and aligned to various celestial bodies. This triangular pattern of the towers, mimicked by the triangular windows, stilled the swell so the gravity waves could mix with the electromagnetic waves.

Apparently I, as the frog-being, was at one of three main towers. The other small towers were like reinforcement stations, helping to set the pattern.

The inside of the Atlantean tower reminded me of our 21st century optical telescopes, some of which I'd photographed at Kitt Peak in Arizona. Like our modern-day observatories, this tall, domed tower with a room at the top was located in a remote area on a forested mountaintop.

But here the similarity ended. The Atlantean tower did not hold finely polished mirrors in exact relationship to one another. This tower held a huge spider that grasped a crystal and a small frog that constantly realigned a ball floating in deep blue light. In addition, it was not used to observe, but to beam down energy from the stars to the Earth.

"How long have you studied to learn to have this job?" asked Lynn.

"How long?" I attempted a reply. "Somehow, if I think of suns, I think I can do it." Obviously time wasn't the same kind of concept it is today. "Let's see," I said. "Time is measured by when the sun is in a certain place. How many times has it been there? I say six. Six times comes to mind."

"Are you male or female?" asked Lynn.

"I'm not sure," was my answer.

In *The Camino*, Shirley MacLaine describes her own experiences as an androgynous being, having the characteristics of both male and female. In her Atlantis experience, she saw how she had separated into two bodies of opposite genders.

In my hypnosis session on Atlantis, while describing the androgynous pixie-faced frog being, my hand kept moving. Automatically, like an extension of his own nervous system, the frog fingers kept moving the ball. Sun at the horizon, moon almost mid-heaven. Although he could not see them inside the tower, he felt them, knew their force in his body. The repelling and attracting of their gravitational fields vibrated within him. As the relationship of the heavenly bodies changed—and they were constantly changing—his long, well-padded fingers tenderly made the minuscule movements that changed the relationship of the ball with the basin, all of it permeated by deep indigo light.

It took a lot of concentration to correctly align the gold stripes that controlled the Crystal. "I have to make sure—perhaps something to do with sunlight," I said. "It has something to do with the direction. I have to keep it aligned all the time. It's like a compass."

A compass works by floating a metal (iron) in a liquid. Because the iron is a magnet, it points towards magnetic north.

The ball with the gold stripe was similar to a compass in that it also floated and was also used for direction. However, whereas the iron in a compass floats in a liquid, the blue egg-shaped ball floated in blue light.

While suspended, the ball felt the way a magnet feels when it's repelled by another magnet. The light had a thick quality to it, similar to a gel.

"There's also a control panel behind," I said, "but the most important thing underneath the spider is this ball that floats."

"What would happen if you don't keep it aligned as it's supposed to be?" asked Lynn.

"We'd just lose power," I answered, as if it should be obvious. "It's not like nowadays. It's that the waves are propagated in certain patterns, and they depend upon the interaction between the sun and the moon and the Earth and various other electromagnetic influences. We have to keep this in the field correctly."

Then I laughed. "For my conscious mind, it's silly to have a human being doing something like that. Nowadays we'd have a machine." However, in many ways the Atlantean system was better than our present technology because the small androgynous frog-being could feel the field in his body. He loved what he was doing—being within and a part of the celestial energy force. The field coursed through him to the ball that controlled the Crystal.

When he was perfectly aligned, a feeling similar to our feeling of ecstasy lighted his being. It was that feeling we have when we listen to inspiring music, when our spirits soar like a great eagle in air currents over the mountains. His dark eyes glistened with the beauty of it.

Lynn asked me what symbol would be an appropriate reminder of this information. I said a gold Capricorn symbol. Gold was important, and the constellation Capricorn was important to us at that time.

"Give us a sense of the kind of person you are," said Lynn.

I giggled. I could see the frog-being springing around in the tower on its long frog legs. When it would leap, it would remain suspended in the air for a long time. "I guess gravity doesn't hold me as tightly as gravity does now," I said, amazed. "I can sort of leap about—I'm not tied to the Earth."

"Yes. Tell me about the . . ." began Lynn.

"Oh, we can levitate!" I interrupted.

"Ahhh!" exclaimed Lynn.

The frog-being hovered beside the long legs of the spider. He lifted to the triangular windows under the domed roof of the tower, flexed his legs and then shot to the other side of the room over the body of the spider. Under him, the Crystal, nestled on the spider's back, glistened with an emerald glow. A bank of multi-colored lights flickered along the wall under the triangular windows. The tower hummed.

When Lynn told me to go to the next significant event, I saw a crack of brilliant light open like a pie shape from the middle of my body in the tower, out into the air outside. It didn't make sense. At first I couldn't comprehend just what I was experiencing.

"That's what it is," I cried out when I finally understood.

"When I leave, I just leave. I don't get into something and go— or walk."

It was as if I had been in the frog-being and now I was out. A crack like a wedge had opened up the ordered molecules, and I was out of the animal and in the daylight.

"It's . . . as if we can go in and out [of bodies] with the Light," I said.

When I'd left the body of the frog-being, I no longer perceived with my senses. It was similar to my experience in the first lifetime regression when I'd found myself a light beam. When I left the body of the frog-being, I became pure Light again without a sense-based understanding of life. That was why I saw only Light.

"I have a feeling it's a rejuvenation place," I added. "It's like going to sleep, only, after you finish working, you go to the Light and rejuvenate for awhile. It's where we dance to light that is healing to us. It's this temple of healing."

I saw different colors of light, mainly reds and yellows. There were people dancing in these lights which shone from behind them. Their shadows played on a large stone wall in front of them.

To a being like my present self who lives in a body that will die, among people and animals who die, to contemplate a life without death and without sleep, took a real stretch of the imagination.

As a symbol that would represent this experience of rejuvenation in the Light, I saw the Hopi stick figure, Kokopelli, a tousle-haired dancing person with a flute, except that the image I saw was without the flute. Kokopelli would be a reminder of how important it is to care for the temple we've been given—our bodies—because "You can't do anything if you aren't keeping yourself healthy and tuned."

It was much more important than the pursuit of money and the many other things that seem so much more important today. "We don't balance ourselves," I said. "We forget about the sunlight. We forget about air. We forget about our heritage and our destiny."

19

Snake Transportation

Next Lynn asked me to go to the most significant event of this experience. Immediately I saw people in distress, with rubble everywhere. There had been a great disaster. Huge rocks were strewn about. Where there had been trees, there were now boulders. Dust rose from the wreckage.

I heard myself moaning. I was a young woman dressed in clothes similar to an East Indian sari. With me was my son, a dark-haired little boy. We huddled on the steps of a temple, looking out over the desolation surrounding us. There had been large-scale destruction of our world. This must have been one of the first upheavals of Atlantis because there was still land left.

There were other people with us on the steps of the temple. They weren't fighting or angry. As with many natural disasters, they were temporarily numb. Those who could were helping those less fortunate.

As I experienced this scene, I was surprised to discover that at the same time I expected to die, I found myself flying in space. I wondered if I had died and was now traveling out of my body. I also wondered, since I had already learned that we rejuvenated instead of dying, how I could be so many different people at once—the wanton Atlantean scientist who formulated the Crystal technology, the pixie-faced frog-like being that controlled the

Crystal, a mother looking over the desolation of earth upheavals, and a being flying through space.

It appeared that I was some kind of over-soul that inhabited different bodies at the same time. It was like reading a number of books at once or like switching back and forth through a number of programs with the remote while watching television. Each of the books or programs represented a different life body that the over-soul experienced.

It was as if we had programmed ahead of time that when the break-up occurred, the over-souls would leave for safety lands. The moaning of the woman was a signal to me that it was time to separate myself from her and the other bodies I worked with in Atlantis and depart.

"It seems as if some of us went to Egypt," I said, "but we didn't walk. We flew!" I saw about a dozen balls of light jettisoned like human cannonballs from the breaking Atlantis. We landed in Egypt, which looked like a lighted-up floating island. In the short time we spun through space, I floated above the dark morass of breaking earth pieces that was Atlantis.

I said that it was better than the rockets nowadays because it was an individual system. To understand the phenomenon of instant transportation, it was important to remember that we weren't the kind of people we are today.

"It's the sense of using that energy that enables the semi-solid type of body to be encapsulated and transported very quickly. It's something that we fashioned in the Earth."

I looked down at a tunnel or hole in the earth that looked like the mouth of a snake. It even had two fangs in the upper jaw. To be instantly transported to the safety lands in Egypt, it appeared that I had to let myself fall into the snake's mouth.

Again and again I repeated the memory of the scene with the snake's jaws opened below me. I remembered falling into the snake's mouth, a sense of darkness and then being catapulted up from the breaking Atlantis into space. While I flew, I looked down at the Earth from space as if I was in a modern-day aircraft, except that I was not in a vehicle. I was like a spinning individual cannonball of light speeding above the Earth with a handful of beings like myself. Our journey was almost instantaneous. We landed in Egypt, which looked like a lighted-up floating intact island. It was as if we had programmed ahead of time that when the break-up occurred, we would be in Egypt.

Over and over I tried to comprehend what I was seeing, and then I understood.

"The Earth works *with* us!" I exclaimed.

"It *agrees* to work with us—there's an *agreement* between us and the forces in the Earth. It [the Earth] has consciousness."

What an unusual concept. Today, we see the Earth as something to manipulate. We *use* it. There is no sense of cooperation, never mind an agreement between us and the forces of nature. We don't consider that the natural world has consciousness.

However, in Atlantis we interacted with elements of the natural world. Whereas today we would force natural elements to create machines, at that time we worked with plants, animals, minerals and metals to accomplish tasks. The various natural elements volunteered or were selected by us because of their innate functions.

For example, the spider's ability to hold and suspend was perfect for carrying the Crystal. The frog's sticky, receptive fingers, plus its inherent receptivity to alterations in the life force through the pineal at the crown of its head, were invaluable for maintaining a constant awareness of the gravitational interaction between the sun, moon, and other heavenly bodies.

In addition, the Crystal, a mineral, and the metal of the gold stripes on the egg-shaped ball and on the rim of the basin consciously worked with us. In the same way, the ceramic tower, forged of minerals, agreed to work with us. Each element was chosen for its inherent characteristics that made the crystal energy source.

Even the woman moaning in the rubble after the earthquake was a element of nature that my Light body worked with to produce the information that the time had come to move to safety lands.

I explained how we knew where to land when we were jettisoned. "We don't coordinate by latitude and longitude. We coordinate through . . . almost like a thought address *with* the Earth. The Earth thinks with us! We're friendlier with the Earth."

The snake was also an earthly being. It had the valuable ability to throw its body when it made a strike. This ability to strike was used for propulsion, to catapult the Atlanteans to their thought-address destinations.

How fascinating. It was transportation by snake propulsion. I remembered the snake carried by the eagle that I'd seen on my bicycle trip, the great wings silhouetted against the rising sun with the snake curled below. It had looked like a flying snake. No wonder this image had moved me so deeply. It had awakened the memory of snake transportation in Atlantis. No wonder I had felt like a compass within me had been set. By following the direction of my inner compass, which had been set by the image of the flying snake, I had finally, more than twenty years later, arrived at the destination of unraveling the mystery. The flying snake represented the Atlantean method of instant transportation.

"So I end up in this place that seems to be Egypt because it has sand, and we build another place to keep a Crystal," I said in the hypnosis.

20

The Great Pyramid

To my surprise, the new place that we built to keep the Crystal was the Great Pyramid. The plant life in Egypt depended on a more cyclical supply of water and therefore was not always consistently green as it had been in Atlantis.

However, our association with the natural world in Egypt hadn't been as long as it had in Atlantis. Therefore, the structure we built in Egypt, modeled on the tower in Atlantis, was built in a way that was coarser than the way we cooperated with nature in Atlantis.

To activate the Great Pyramid so that it functioned like an Atlantean tower, we had only to find and attach the capstone to the top. The capstone, which must be about 18 feet tall, is not on the Great Pyramid. "The reason why the capstone is off is to keep it safe," I said. "It was blown off—kept off. If it was ever put on, it would start to vibrate again, and people wouldn't know what to do with it."

Amazingly, I was saying that the Atlanteans had incorporated the design of the Crystal-powered tower into the design of the Great Pyramid. Using the coarser rocks in Egypt, they had fashioned a structure that would last through the millennia.

I felt that the capstone, should it be found, held an Atlantean-type crystal. Should the capstone be placed correctly on top of the

Great Pyramid, the pyramid would begin to hum and vibrate as had the tower in Atlantis.

I also said that the Great Pyramid, as well as the tower in Atlantis—and the human body—were meant to operate on the same energy dynamic. In all three, the Crystal (or pineal) was used to integrate celestial energy such as gravity (or sunlight) with terrestrial energy such as electromagnetism.

When the pineal was properly activated in our bodies, we too would hum with celestial energy. We would be healed via the soul, our physical aligned with the Light body. This was the reason why I had been told that all of us in the modern world needed to be in natural sunlight more often and to live more by natural rhythms.

In the same way, when the capstone containing the Atlantean crystal was placed on top of the Great Pyramid, it, too, would hum with energy.

However, it was not yet time for the pyramid to hum with energy. "The spot has to be correct in relationship to certain stars," I said. Then the swell in the gravity waves could be stilled and integrated with electromagnetic waves in the same manner as in the tower in Atlantis.

I was referring to the Precession of the Equinoxes. Our solar system only *appears* to be moving in exactly the same place compared to distant stars. Actually, over the millennia, the Earth moves in respect to distant stars. Evidently the main three towers in Atlantis had been built at exactly the correct places for the gravitational energy to be ordered against distant stars. In Atlantis this had had something to do with the constellation Capricorn.

The ability to harness the power of far-away stars such as Arcturus was possible only from certain places on Earth and at certain times. The next place that this power could be used would be at the Great Pyramid. Then it would be possible to integrate gravity with electromagnetism as it had been in Atlantis.

Interestingly, in *The Giza Power Plant*, author and engineer Christopher Dunn shows how the Great Pyramid could have been built as a machine that resonates with the Earth. Based on his calculations as an engineer, he believes the Great Pyramid was used to create power in the past. The information in my hypnosis sessions says that the Great Pyramid will be used in the future. He talks about masers and hydrogen generators. I talk about gravity and electromagnetism. However, we both agree that the structure was built to resonate with the Earth.

In my memories of the Atlantean purpose of the Great Pyramid, when the time is again right, the Great Pyramid will be in correspondingly the same place, compared to the distant stars, as the tower was in Atlantis. This time is coming up soon. To harness gravity waves, three towers or pyramids are needed. The other two main pyramids will be in the Yucatan and in Atlantis, the latter rising with the upcoming earth changes according to the Edgar Cayce readings.

Lynn asked me, "And how will you know when it is ordered correctly? What are the parameters, the characteristics? Has that happened yet?"

"No," I answered emphatically.

"It won't happen until the millennium, when people are kind again.

"It shouldn't happen! It's meant to *not* happen until after 2011!"

"And what is the reason for your needing to reconnect with this old, old memory now, in terms of the unfolding path that you're following in your life?"

"My sense is to gather the faithful," I said, and that was when my vision, described in Chapter Five, The Vision, began. I saw young people whose heads were bowed, kneeling on one knee. They began to glow with a golden light and then stood up. They were people of all countries, races, and religions throughout the world. There were hundreds of thousands of them. They were sincere people, the hope of the world. Drawn to the pyramids, they had knowledge of an ability we had developed in Atlantis that would provide the Earth with energy that would work with the Earth rather than destroy it.

There would be a new world. It would use a different power source, a technology that depended upon an *agreement* with the Earth. It used gravity and electromagnetism, enhancing rather than destroying the natural world. This technology had been left in the Great Pyramid for the upcoming generation to rediscover and use. They had a memory of it in their unconscious minds.

During the time the pyramid was being built, they had taken on the task to reincarnate when the Earth hung precariously close to destruction. That time was now.

"There is hope!" I exclaimed.

"There *really* is hope! And everything around us that's so dark and frightening just falls away. It's not terrible. It just falls away. And these faithful just keep tuned to that golden spot. That's all they have to do. They're going to wake up.

"This is the next race being born."

We had entered as light beams, in tune with God, able to travel anywhere in the universe, aware of our heavenly purpose. That was the First Root Race. Next we had become entrapped in the physical—translucent, wisps of smoke, a thought form, unable to leave the Earth, trapped. That was the Second Root Race.

In Atlantis we had become the Third Root Race, simultaneously existing in different bodies at once in an agreement with nature, capable of levitation and instant transportation.

In a future session I would explore how we became the Fourth Root Race—human beings—beings that appear to be animals, but during sleep, between lifetimes, and in their unconscious minds are still aware of their true heritage and destiny as Light Beings.

Hypnotized on Lynn's recliner with my mangled, bruised heel elevated, my unconscious mind swam with a view of life that was so large that my conscious mind could hardly envision what it saw. My experience in Atlantis was so unlike anything that I had expected. My reasons to fear facing Atlantis had proved to be far different than anything I had imagined before I came into the session.

The Great Pyramid

Lynn asked me, "And these concerns you had had about possibly having something to pay back from Atlantis, or some guilt there (my dream of the wanton Atlantean scientist)—is there anything to that, or is that a misunderstanding?"

"No," I replied. "It was responsibility! I have a responsibility! I have something I have to do. *I have got to get on with it!*"

After the session I went to my local library and picked up a copy of *Secrets of the Great Pyramid* by Peter Tompkins, the book that had fascinated me during my college years after I'd returned from my bicycle trip.

I was especially interested in a passage about the top of the pyramid, the place where the capstone should be. I remembered that even with the capstone missing, there was some sort of strong force at the top of the pyramid

I found the passage on pages 278 and 279. One of the many visitors to the Great Pyramid was the British inventor Sir W. Siemens. Standing on the flat top of the pyramid, Siemens noted that when he raised his arm with his index finger extended, he felt a prickling sensation in his finger. Then when he tried to drink from a wine bottle, he noticed a slight electric shock on his lips.

Siemens made a Leyden jar out of his wine bottle by coating it with damp newspaper. A Leyden jar is an electric capacitor, something that condenses an electric charge. By holding the makeshift Leyden jar over his head, Siemens was able to concentrate such an electric charge that sparks flew from the top of the bottle.

At the sight of the sparkles escaping from the mouth of the jar, Siemens' Arab guides became afraid. They thought he had cast a spell and was practicing witchcraft. When one of the guides tried to grab Siemens' companion, Siemens brought the jar down from over his head and pointed the mouth of the jar at the guide. The guide received such a shock that he passed out and fell to the ground.

From this account, it appears that the Pyramid is made in such a way that there is a build-up of electrical charge at its apex. If the capstone truly does contain an Atlantean Crystal, as my hypnosis said, it is conceivable that, should the capstone be put in place, it could set some kind of powerful energy in motion.

I assume the Golden Ones or the Fifth Root Race will know where to find the capstone and how to levitate it to the top of the Pyramid. I have a feeling that it is in what Cayce calls the "Hall of Records," which is not supposed to be opened until the advent of the Fifth Root Race.

While I was at the library, I also saw another book on ancient Egypt called *The Message of the Sphinx*, by Graham Hancock and Robert Bauval. It caught my interest because the authors believe that part of the reason for the construction of the Sphinx is to emphasize the constellation Leo, its celestial counterpart. Leo faces the constellation Orion, which is acknowledged in ancient Egyptian texts as the Star Gate through which the pharaoh must travel to become free of our planet and gain immortality.

It sounded like the Star Gate in my hypnosis sessions, the doorway between different solar systems, which could be traversed only in our original light beam form.

When I looked at a star chart, I was surprised to discover that Arcturus lies behind and below Leo. It made me wonder if the ancient builders of the Sphinx and the three Great Pyramids chose to emphasize Leo because, by coincidence, it lies between Orion and Arcturus. What if the Sphinx is telling us that "we became half beasts, half Light Beings. The way out is through Orion. Behind us is home, Arcturus."

21

When We Were Gods

Because I was afraid of remaining fat forever after my session of admonishment with the archangels, I quickly wrote the manuscript and was back with it in Lynn's office in a month. It was rough—*very* rough. There was one chapter written in outline form, in pencil. Some passages rambled. Others that begged extensive treatment were noted with one sparse sentence. There were spelling and grammatical errors as well as typos everywhere. But it had a beginning, a middle and, most importantly, an end. And I had it in my hands—two thick binders full of typed pages.

The archangels were right. Although I still wondered if I believed any of this weird stuff, the thought that I might be fat for the rest of my life kept me tied to the computer. They definitely had leverage!

To my relief, after I was hypnotized, the Brotherhood let me know that I had done well. The middle one of the stern men handed me a sheaf of papers representing the manuscript as if he'd just finished reading it. His face—anyway, what I could see of it under the hood—shone with joy and satisfaction. It was as if he said, "Little sister, you have done well." But, of course, the exchange was entirely telepathic. He let me know that I shouldn't worry that it was not yet perfect. I also was able to see more of his face than ever before, because his hood was half raised. Surprisingly, he looked Mexican, with swarthy skin and fleshy lips. His wide mouth smiled broadly. It made me feel good as well as relieved to know he was happy.

Only recently I've realized what the archangels were trying to tell me all along: my greatest happiness comes from helping others. By sharing this information instead of keeping it to myself, I may help others to gain a better understanding of life.

After the Brotherhood approved the rough manuscript, I began to discover some of the missing pieces of the story—how we had become the Fourth Root Race, the animal-like form in which we presently find ourselves. Moreover, I would find out that both the Creationists and the Evolutionists are right—we were created in God's image, and our animal bodies have evolved.

The previous session had ended in Egypt. Lynn and I decided to return there. After I was hypnotized, the most outstanding feature in my first memory perception was a colossus of a man, imposingly attractive, standing before me with his feet apart and arms folded across his chest.

He wore a headdress that rested on his shoulders and came partly down his torso, of the type seen on drawings and statues of many Egyptian pharaohs. The headdress shone with gold and black stripes that were arranged diagonally along the side of his head, making it look as if sunbeams shone from around his face. His name was "Amon."

Resting in the chair in Lynn's office, I had a feeling of deep, deep love for Amon, almost to the point of wanting to cry because he was so beautiful. Physically he was amazing—well-muscled and bronze skinned, wearing a short tunic made of gold about mid-thigh in length. He wore a gold belt at his waist with a gold band around the hem of the tunic skirt. The whole outfit was fashioned of gold leaves layered over each other. There was also gold hanging over both his shoulders, like epaulets. Around each smoothly muscled upper arm he sported a gold band with a gold tongue that hung down about an inch below the band. I could see his muscled bronze legs and then gold boots with perhaps wings on the back of them.

I had the feeling that he supervised a construction project because there was a large ramp behind him with workers on it. He stood above me on steps leading up to the ramp. I stood below him on the steps. I wore a Grecian style dress of a diaphanous white fabric with a gold rope around my waist. I had golden hair tied up with a gold rope and appeared to be bare-footed. My face was high-cheek-boned but longer than my face in this present lifetime, which is more round and square.

Amon and I faced each other. Behind him the building under construction appeared to be made of golden stones or else the stones were covered in gold. Today we call it the Great Pyramid.

I saw the structure rise out of a grassy plane. It was not as we find the Great Pyramid today—surrounded by a barren sandy desert. It was more fertile, grassy and green. However, it was more like a grassland than a forest. Because the land flooded yearly, grasses grew in the sandy soil.

Amon supervised the construction of this structure. The ramp is presently known as the Grand Gallery. Behind it was a building that today is called the King's Chamber. Today they are both within the pyramid, having been covered by the outer rocks which presently make the pyramid form around them.

However, I was seeing them during their construction and therefore they appeared to be a large long building slanted like a ramp, with another building behind it on top of a foundation about one third the height of the present Great Pyramid. The whole area looked like a present-day plaza in the middle of a large city, except, of course, that this was in the middle of a green, grassy area. The rest of the pyramid would be added around the foundation and inner structures later.

One of the great mysteries surrounding the three Great Pyramids is that they are made of monolithic stones, some of which are 70 tons in weight, for example, the 70-ton boulders making up the ceiling of the King's Chamber. How were they transported? In many places, the many-tonned boulders making up the Great Pyramid are fitted together so perfectly that a knife blade cannot pass between them—an engineering feat we cannot yet replicate. Because the three Great Pyramids have no drawings, hieroglyphics or embellishments of any kind within or without, it is a great mystery as to how they were built and for what purpose.

There are also many smaller pyramids in Egypt that are more poorly built than the Great Pyramids, as well as structures and temples built of smaller stones. Unlike the Great Pyramids, many of these structures are embellished with picturesque stone carvings, paintings and hieroglyphics that describe a method of building pyramids involving armies of slaves pulling huge rocks up earthen ramps on oiled skids.

Because of these hieroglyphics, archeologists assume all the ancient structures, including the three Great Pyramids, were built using slaves and oiled skids. However, although this could explain how huge rocks were moved, it cannot account for the 70-ton boulders fitting together with such perfect precision.

However, as I was about to find out, according to my past life memories, these structures definitely were not made by dragging monolithic stones on oiled skids.

The boulders flew through the air. One at a time the stones flipped end over end, and then wham!, they'd land exactly where they were meant to be, exactly in the shape that perfectly fit the space where they belonged.

I realized that they had been levitated in a way similar to the way the frog-being had levitated in the tower. It wasn't that the stones were lifted and carried. It was that the atoms were actually rearranged. The stones were dematerialized and rematerialized exactly where they belonged. When the atoms were rearranged during rematerialization, the material was slightly changed because of pressure put on it during the process.

The Great Pyramid was an Atlantean relic. As in Atlantis, the stones had an address with the Earth. We, the Atlanteans who fled to Egypt when the earth changes began, made an address with nature that positioned the stones exactly in the correct place. That was why the stones fit so perfectly together.

There are also a couple of temples in Egypt made of monolithic stones that fit perfectly together, some in jig-saw-puzzle patterns.

Some of the megalithic stones even bend around corners or fit perfectly over previously existing land formations as if they were molded. I was finding out that they had been molded, using the Atlantean ability to work powerfully with the physical through an agreement with nature.

There is an ancient Arab legend that says that the pyramids were built by supernatural beings called the jinn, entities who could enter animal bodies and even enter stones. I believe this is a memory of the Third Root Race and their ability to work in an agreement with nature.

Although to us today it appears unbelievable that the stones could be dematerialized and rematerialized in this manner, I had already seen myself jettisoned in a similar manner from Atlantis to Egypt when Atlantis began to break up. Therefore, based on my previous memory, 70-ton boulders flying through the air did not seem that unusual to me. It was just the way things were done.

When Lynn asked me where the stones came from, I saw them cut out of a quarry nearby. This stone was chosen because it had quartz in it. Although my conscious mind could consider that the stones could dematerialize and rematerialize, I simply can't believe what I saw in the quarry. The stones seemed to separate themselves out of the solid rock into blocks, just as stone would split during an earthquake. No machinery was used. It was evidently another example of our agreement with nature, similar to how we had worked with the Crystal in Atlantis.

Another one of the mysteries surrounding the three Great Pyramids is the question of *when* they were built. Conventional scholarship has it that because the three Great Pyramids are the largest and most precisely built, they must be the quintessence of the pyramid builders' art, the crowning glory of pyramid-building technologies. Therefore, archeologists conclude that the three Great Pyramids had to be the most recently built pyramids in Egypt. They logically surmise that the smaller pyramids, which are much more poorly built and have relatively smaller stones, must have been earlier attempts at the art of pyramid building. Based on how human beings learn now, the archeologists conclude that the pyramid builders increased their abilities until, suddenly, they built three colossal monuments that were superior in every way to the "practice" structures.

I was about to discover that the three large pyramids had to have been built first. The ancient Egyptians must have built the smaller, more poorly-built pyramids in an attempt to imitate the three Great Pyramids which they had found already existing in their land.

Above Amon and me flew a large eagle with a human-type face. The eagle's feathers were duplicates of the same gold leaves that made up Amon's outfit. The eagle was Ra. Interestingly, in his own past life readings, Edgar Cayce discovered he had been Ra during his Egyptian incarnation. According to *Grolier's Encyclopedia*, Ra or Re was the Egyptian sun god represented in the hieroglyphics by a man with a falcon's head surrounded by the disc of the sun, symbol of Ra. Coincidentally, flying snakes appear on the sun disc, which is decorated with two serpents set in the middle of a pair of outspread wings.

Ra was Amon's superior, ultimately responsible for the construction of the Pyramid as well as many other projects. Amon was uneasy because he wanted to make a good impression. As Ra swooped over the construction, his long golden wings twisted and turned as he rode the air currents, the long wing tips spread wide. He literally watched every detail like a hawk.

At that time we still had the ability to go in and out of bodies and to manipulate the physical to our liking. The eagle body was merely a convenient form for Ra to take when he wanted to survey construction progress. He was also capable of taking on other body forms, altering those forms and rejuvenating in the Light as had the frog-being/Atlantean scientist that controlled the Crystal in Atlantis.

The gold in all our outer coverings—Amon's outfit, my golden belt, Ra's gold-leaved feathers—were vital for instant transportation and levitation as well as for the ability to go in and out of bodies. They functioned in the same way that the gold stripes had interacted between the ball and basin that controlled the Crystal in Atlantis.

"I also have the images of gold carts and beasts that fly," I said in the hypnosis session. "A lot of shiny, golden stuff. We are really different people. God, how different! The place reeks of power—over life, over the physical—just an *amazing* power over the physical world [for example] ... they're eagles. They *make* themselves what they want to be."

After the eagle swooped down over the ramp/Grand Gallery and acknowledged Amon standing with arms crossed, the bird flew away. With Ra gone, Amon and I were more at ease. Amon took off his headdress and threw it on the ground. He was angry with something I had done. However, he didn't actually take the headdress off and fling it to the ground. He sent me a visual image of the feeling. Throwing the headdress down was the most appropriate mental picture to symbolize his feeling of anger and frustration with me.

I had somehow disappointed him. Because I had arrived late at the construction site, he feared I was falling back into my old ways. It was the old problem from Atlantis—I had confided secret information on the workings of the Crystal to the wrong people.

"Are you a worker there?" asked Lynn.

"No," I replied, "I'm a goddess."

A goddess. I was a goddess! What was that about? I searched my mind to understand what I meant by the word "goddess," and then I realized that I had used the word to mean that we still knew ourselves to be made in God's image and therefore were gods and goddesses. It was as if we had all been gods and goddesses at one time—as long as we were still in touch with our Light selves. Those beings who could no longer go in and out of bodies or rejuvenate in the Light were no longer gods and goddesses.

Because Amon and I were very familiar with each other, he felt comfortable sending me these very personal images. I seemed to be both his sister and his lover. Some part of me cried inside, but on the outside I kept my chin up and maintained my haughty stance as if to say, "Who does he think he is to make this judgment of me?"

Nonetheless, despite my outward arrogance, I feared that he might be right that I could fall back into my old ways, the equivalent of which today would be to be drunk, stoned, and compulsively sexual—in other words, vulnerable to manipulation.

While maintaining the haughty stance, I sent him a mental image of falling at his feet and sobbing in supplication for his understanding and forgiveness. I also sent him a mental picture of my work in the temple where I had been helping individuals who were incapable of moving in and out of bodies to purify themselves.

Many of the Light Beings who had lost their ability to move in and out of bodies were now permanently locked into matter, some of which were grotesque mixtures of animals. Today we remember them as mythological creatures such as mermaids (half man, half fish), Pegasus (half horse, half eagle) and griffins (half lion, half eagle).

The grotesque animal forms were cleansed in a Temple of Sacrifice, similar to our present-day hospitals. I explained that the chamber in the Great Pyramid presently known as the Pit was the place where the appendages were removed from the beasts, in procedures similar to present-day surgical operations. The Pit is a subterranean chamber built into the bedrock directly below the apex of the Great Pyramid. "People are cleansed and beautiful, and hope is everywhere," I said.

The healing process was continued in the Temple Beautiful, which corresponded to the Atlantean rejuvenation temples described in Chapter 18, The Tower and the Crystal. I worked in the Temple Beautiful, attempting to atone for my mistake of allowing the Crystal information to fall into the wrong hands. My present responsibility—to awaken the Golden Ones as we begin the 21st century—also came out of this need to atone for my errors in Atlantis.

It appeared that during the final days of Atlantis, one of the Great Pyramid's functions was for healing. I also had the sense that the orientation to the stars was important, because lights, especially those of golden and red colors, were used to heal the physical.

After I telepathically showed Amon my work in the temple, he softened, visibly glowing. I saw myself leap up to him as he telepathically called me up to him. He held me to his chest. I actually melted right into him. We were one. I felt his boundless love for me and returned my love for him. The feeling of love was amazingly powerful.

Suddenly I knew that the Great Pyramids had not been built by the ancient Egyptians. They had to have been built by Atlanteans or similar beings. It was so obvious. The hieroglyphic writing and pictures were made by beings who used language—people like ourselves.

I realized that the Great Pyramid did not have any writing in or on it because it had been built by beings *who did not use language* to communicate. Like Amon and my goddess self, they conversed telepathically, they sent image bundles to each other. The beings who built the three Great Pyramids didn't put writing on their walls because they did not speak—or write. Even though they occasionally used the vibrational power of sound in working with the physical, they didn't communicate with words.

Furthermore, there was no use in making drawings of the bodies the gods and goddesses took upon themselves since these ancient beings, who could infinitely rejuvenate themselves, knew they were actually eternal Light Beings. The occasional animal-like bodies they used served only a temporary purpose—to view, to build, or to help. They did not identify with these bodies. They were not an eagle or a man with a golden tunic or a woman wearing a white gown tied with a golden belt—or a frog or a spider. These were just bodies they took on temporarily. They knew who they were—beings made in the image of God. To make a picture in stone of their temporary embodiment would be absurd—they were not animals, and they knew it. They were Light Beings—gods and goddesses.

It was obvious, then, that the hieroglyphics and pictures had been made by beings who used words for communication, beings like ourselves. These beings came *after* the more powerful telepathic builders of the original three Great Pyramids.

Those who came *after* the gods and goddesses had made the poorly-built smaller pyramids in an attempt to imitate the three Great Pyramids. Without the ability to levitate and instantly transport matter, they had had to resort to armies of slaves, earthen ramps, and oiled skids.

It was these beings, human beings, who used language to communicate, who told the stories of their memories of the gods and goddesses in hieroglyphics, paintings, and stone carvings. It was these beings who depicted the gods with solar discs on their heads.

The Bible says that after the Flood (probably the cataclysm that destroyed Atlantis), God was concerned that man should never again be so powerful that God would want to destroy humankind. Therefore, God gave man language so that we could never again communicate easily with each other. We were made less powerful by language.

Language? What was that? Who needed it when you could project whatever you wanted, even to the point of levitation or instantaneous transportation or golden body forms?

It is difficult for us to imagine the type of beings we were when we were gods.

"Power, immense power," I said under hypnosis.

"[Today] we don't even come close to it. Almost all our power is just to break things. This [power we once had] is the power to create things. It's very different—very strong creative power."

When we were gods, we knew how to rearrange the atoms in stone and move our Light bodies into and out of matter. We could change existing animals into beasts of our own making. The bodies we made were perfectly beautiful. We never died. Whenever we needed to rest, we returned to our true Light selves and were rejuvenated.

154

So how and why did we become the animal-like, relatively powerless little beings we presently find ourselves? I was about to find out.

22

Death is the New Thing

Modern scientists are amazed that the three Great Pyramids are oriented exactly to the points of the compass. The Great Pyramid is also proportionately an exact replica of the northern hemisphere: the relationship of its height to circumference is exactly the same relationship that the height of the Earth from equator to pole is to the circumference of the equator.

In addition, the Great Pyramid is situated exactly on the 30th degree of latitude with such accuracy that it is as if it was placed there by a being looking down at it from the sky. There is some speculation that the pyramid was built as a monument to memorialize these measurements for future generations.

But from what I was seeing, it was absurd that power beings such as the gods and goddesses would have gone to the trouble to build these monuments as an eternal measuring stick. The Great Pyramid was built at the 30th parallel of latitude because that's the exact location it needed in order to operate properly. It was built in an exact proportion with the Earth because that's the proportion it needed in order to resonate correctly for its function. And what was its main function?

During the time we were gods and goddesses, its main function was to integrate the bodies of the Light Beings who had become trapped in physical forms, with the natural world to create the Fourth Root Race, presently known as the human race.

At the time when we entered the Earth as Light Beings, our leader, Amilius, who later became the Christ, had not become trapped in the physical. With Gabriel and Michael, he was one of the members of the Great White Brotherhood, part of the angelic hierarchy. He and the Brotherhood had been watching us playing with our toys—the material world. They feared we would no longer want to free ourselves and return to our true purpose with the Creator.

Amilius saw us as imprisoned but oblivious to our precarious situation. We had forgotten how we cried and wailed to go home when first trapped by the physical. We had forgotten how ashamed we were to have separated ourselves from the Creator. We had even forgotten how lonely we were.

Amilius was afraid we would totally forget our divine heritage and become lost forever. Those of us encased in grotesque mixtures of animal bodies might remain trapped forever. And those of us who were still gods were glorying in our power over the physical, with no desire to return home.

We were drunk on our own power, addicted to the physical. Who cared if we were imprisoned in it? We liked it. We were powerful and important. It felt marvelous.

Nonetheless, Amilius was aware of our perilous situation. He knew we were in danger of permanently severing our ties with the Creator. He looked upon us with compassion. He wanted to free us from the physical, but how could He motivate us to want to escape?

The problem was our free will. We no longer wanted to return to our Light-being state. No one, not even God, could force us to return to our true nature if we did not want to.

What could Amilius do to make beings who had free will want to leave the physical? How could He make us aware of our imprisonment? He noticed that in the physical forms on Earth, there were animals evolving in a separate, albeit God-given, existence from our own. It was a normal part of the animals' development to go through birth and death. What if Amilius gave us death? What if we knew the suffering of disease and misfortune? Would that awaken us from our fascination with the physical? Would it make us want to return to the Creator? Would we begin to awaken from our drunken stupor?

This was the plan, made with cooperation from the Brotherhood, that Amilius followed. He went first to show us the way. He created a modified animal body, the first one called Adam, which means "man made of the red dust of the Earth." He, the being that would one day become the Christ, was the first Adam. By becoming this man, Amilius entered the prison with us. He would show us the way out from the inside.

This modified animal body was the Fourth Root Race, the human race. It would know death and suffer. Between lifetimes and in its dreams and meditations, it would return to its spirit self to assimilate the experiences during its lifetimes. Over and over again the soul-body would take on a new physical body. In each incarnation it would learn lessons. It would try to find glory in power but only encounter failure, discovering its greatest happiness in aligning more closely with the purposes of the soul body.

Eventually, purified through suffering, the physical being would want only to be one with the Creator. Then the animal-like beings would live a life in which they proved to themselves that their first priority was to follow God's will against all temptations. They would also put others before themselves. For Amilius, this culminated in the lifetime as Jesus of Nazareth. It was in that lifetime that He finally showed us the way out of the prison of the physical. He had transcended the need for the lessons of suffering in the modified animal body. He no longer needed nor was controlled by death. Paradoxically, He became free by totally giving up His will and power to the Creator. That was why Jesus said, "I am the Way," because His life was an example to us of the way to free ourselves.

He had taken on this task at the beginning of the creation of humanity, or the Fourth Root Race. It was as if we had all taken on certain responsibilities at the end of the last age: Amilius to become the Christ and show us the way out of the prison of the physical, the Golden Ones to bring in the Fifth Root Race, myself to awaken them, each of us to do whatever our purpose might be in the drama that was to unfold.

Under hypnosis on December 3, 1996, I relived my experience of the creation of the Fourth Root Race. I was in a dark room, almost like a cave except that it had four sides. I had the impression it was in the underground room built into the bedrock below the Great Pyramid, now called the Pit. Amon was on the left, and I, on the right. A baby was on something like a table between us.

This child was different from anything I, as a goddess, had ever encountered before. For one thing, it was pink. It reminded me of a little piglet—a pet being. Amon and I were very different from the "piglet" baby. We were a more golden people, able to move from body to body. This poor little pet being was stuck in its piglet form. Although we loved it, it was very strange to us.

During the fusion of Light body with animal body, the baby seemed to glow, lighting the room. Hovering above us was the spirit of Amilius. Although I couldn't see Him, as always when I was in His presence, He was recognizable by the overwhelmingly powerful feeling of love that emanated from Him.

I, on the other hand, was scared. It seemed that Amilius had created this helpless pink piglet baby as a physical vehicle for His soul. I was afraid He had gone too far. It seemed like such a harsh step to take. I was afraid for Him—and I was afraid for myself because I knew the rest of us had to follow Amilius' example. I didn't want to become a helpless pink piglet. I loved being a goddess. I didn't want to forget that I was a Light Being.

Moreover, the baby needed so much care. We fed it on honey and nectar. Later, when more like it were created, they could give birth and nurse their babies. But at first, when there were no mothers or fathers, the piglet babies were not born but created in the Pit. They were so much like little animals. It was frightening that this was what Amilius would make Himself and what He would expect us to become.

I saw a grassy place where the baby lived and grew up to young adulthood. It was a nice place, green, with some flowers, some vines, some trees.

Then something truly terrible happened. The young man died. I loved Him, but He died. For the first time I knew grief. I hadn't experienced death before. It was a terrible shock.

We experienced the young man in His dead form because this new being had an alive time and a dead time. So after the grief, we found the human being was not really dead. And again I had the sense that it was the Christ, Amilius.

But after His death, I saw He was back in His original Light form. I realized that it was natural that He existed after death. After all, we were all eternal beings.

Death was the *new* thing.

It not only taught us the limitations of the physical but also gave us the opportunity to learn many lessons because we could experience different lifetimes.

According to Glenn Sanderfur's *Lives of the Master*, based on the Edgar Cayce readings, the Christ had 33 appearances in the Earth in an animal-like human form, starting with Adam. A few others of His Biblical incarnations were as Enoch, Melchizedek, Joseph, and Joshua, until He became Jesus of Nazareth and demonstrated to us that He was now free of the physical because He was no longer bound by death.

We had to follow His example and become animal-like forms like Him, die, and reincarnate until we were filled with yearning to return to God. It was as if Amilius was a very good boss and I trusted Him explicitly. After all, because He was part of the angelic hierarchy, He knew much more than I did. Moreover, I would do anything for Amilius because of His deep love for me and for all of us.

Reliving the scene while hypnotized, I said, "I'm scared—to make this helpless kind of being that also dies. I've never experienced that before, the grief. He [Amilius] knows what He's doing, but I'm scared. Such a drastic type of thing to do."

However, Amilius, out of the body, in the death time, was still Amilius—very powerful and amazingly kind.

Each of the gods and goddesses in turn followed Amilius' example and went into their spirit selves first. Although we reveled in going into and out of bodies, we had to relinquish that ability and remain in the spirit until we were mixed with the animal form. Then, from the experiments being done in the underground chamber in the Pyramid, we each had "little pink piglet things to go into—to become helpless."

The pink piglet people were the Fourth Root Race, created in the Pyramid. In the Pit, those Light Beings who had lost the ability to move in and out of bodies had to make the sacrifice of being surgically divulged of their weird appendages and made, with the cooperation of the nature kingdom, into a standardized body form, today known as the human race. It was a step toward freedom for those who had become permanently enmeshed in grotesque mixtures of animal bodies. They could again move from body to body, but sequentially now, through reincarnation.

Those beings who could still move into and out of bodies—the gods and goddesses—had to relinquish their ties with the many bodies they had "played with" and become enmeshed in this standardized animal form. For the gods and goddesses, it was also a time of sacrifice—to lose the ability to create so powerfully. However, although they could no longer manifest through different bodies at the same time, they could still work with different bodies one at a time, through sequential lifetimes.

"There's this endless . . ."

I sighed, "endless sacrificing. Just this endless, endless, endless having to let go for a greater good. Just like what's coming up again, just endlessly."

In many ways the Bible was the story of this Fourth Root Race and the promise that, by willingly undergoing the suffering of the animal-like body, we could become free and return "home" to oneness with God.

The creation of the Fourth Root Race was a very important step in our return to the Creator. It was the turning point. It was the time when we realized our imprisonment, when we prayed for deliverance, when we asked for God's help. The change to the Fifth Root Race, which I realized was almost upon us, would also require sacrificing on our part.

No wonder Pan wanted so much to be included in the book. It is vitally important that we honor the natural world. The Fourth Root Race could not have been created without an agreement between the natural world and our Light essence. We, the human race, are the ultimate Atlantean agreement with nature.

In the Fourth Root Race, the points of contact between the eternal Light bodies and the mortal animal bodies are at the endocrine gland centers, what we call the chakras or spiritual centers. When the animal body dies, the eternal Light body continues to live as it always has, still does, and always will.

Eventually the Light body will connect with another "piglet body" for another lifetime. Before birth, the Light body or soul hovers over the developing animal body in the mother's womb.

Many mothers report dreams in which they communicate with their unborn children. It is the incoming being's soul or Light body with which the mothers converse. At birth, usually with the first breath, the Light body meshes with the emerging physical body.

I have experienced this myself. As Clair's body was born, the room was permeated with a peachy-golden glow. This was her soul hovering over the emerging gray-blue animal body. At the same time that she cried, the glow in the room disappeared, and her little body turned pink. Her Light body had locked into the animal body at the chakras. She was alive.

Lynn had a question about an earlier comment I had made.

"What is the greater good from which you have to let go?" she asked. "To be free," I replied, "to be free of Satan. To get free of this dark place. And we bring all kinds of information back to the Father. It's exciting. We're His creations. He wants to know what's going on. And we want to get back to see Him, and this is the way we have to do it. It's like we have to walk through a swamp [with snakes and leeches] to get home. We just have to get through it. It seems endless. It's amazing that the Christ feels so loving always. He is huge. His feeling of love—the power—is huge."

It was because of His great love for us that He and the Brotherhood had devised the Fourth Root Race to turn our will so we would free ourselves from the physical. In any case, in the hypnosis session, I then added, "And you know, we're just little guys in this one," meaning that this interaction among Satan, Christ, Gabriel, and Michael was a much larger drama than our own little dilemma of being caught in the physical and returning to the Light. In the Christian mystical tradition, Michael routed the rebellious archangel Lucifer, later known as Satan, from heaven to hell. However, we became caught up in this larger drama when we chose to disobey the will of the Creator, making us vulnerable to Satan's power.

Lynn then asked, "And once Satan is bound, then what?"

"Peace!" I pronounced without hesitation.

"The thousand years?" asked Lynn.

"Peace," I repeated. "Yes. I see pink. And I see that people will be able to love without fear of being punished, hated, or destroyed."

It's a sad comment to make that we live in a world where, if we love the wrong religion, love our family instead of obeying a cruel law or love a person of the wrong color, we may be punished, hated or destroyed.

". . . They will just be able to love," I continued. "And you know, love is being aligned with the God within—that's the goal: the Golden self. These Golden people are loving people.

"That's how you get peace," I said. "You don't get peace with peace treaties. You have to have people who are peaceful and loving. They're the kind of people who know and live that love is its own reward.

"When you have love as its own reward," I concluded, "you aren't greedy anymore.

"So we will have that on Earth."

Evidently the Fifth Root Race will live a fulfillment of love. Therefore, they will be kind and good. They will have no need to justify greed, ruthlessness, cruelty, etc., because they will feel fulfilled within themselves.

This was the future for which the Brotherhood had prepared us when the human race was created. However, once the beings who were permanently stuck in the strange mixtures of animals became human beings, and once the gods and goddesses relinquished their ability to go into and out of bodies to become human beings, the Pyramids eventually became ruins.

"The little piglet people don't really know what to do with it. Even we [who made it] don't know what to do with it. It's pretty. It's nice. But before long it doesn't glow golden anymore. That's what the new ones [the Fifth Root Race] will know how to do—how to make it glow again."

As an afterthought I added, "The Three Pyramids are physical, mental, and spiritual, and one of them has an extra room in it—not necessarily the Great Pyramid." I saw a room in the second (i.e., mental) or middle pyramid.

"Anything on the Hall of Records?" asked Lynn. She was referring to the room that Cayce says contains the Atlantean record of the soul on Earth and the blueprint for the future.

"The capstone is a clue to the Hall of Records. I sure wish I knew where it was—there's something with the capstone. Somebody knows, Lynn," I said. "I mean, why did they put that eye in it, on the dollar bill? Somebody knows."

The American one-dollar bill has an engraving of the Pyramid on it. The capstone, which contains a large, beaming eye, floats above the pyramid. In trance I felt that the eye probably represented the Atlantean Crystal and that someone, somewhere—perhaps among the Masons—already knew the significance of the capstone to the Pyramid.

I continued, "I see actually something like an emerald." I also felt that the capstone was likely buried in the Hall of Records near the Pyramid.

"There's extensive underground [tunnels and chambers]—it might be that where you go into it at the paw [of the Sphinx] is just where you go into it, but it [the Hall of Records] might be somewhere else." Cayce says that the Hall of Records can be accessed through a passageway starting at the right paw of the Sphinx.

"When will the Hall of Records be found?" asked Lynn.

"Do you know there's one in the Yucatan?" I replied.

"A Hall of Records?"

"Yes. Someone is working there quietly without all the fanfare and is very close and doesn't know it."

23

Feathered Serpent

In February 1999, John and I traveled to the Yucatan Peninsula in Mexico. I didn't have any illusions that in two weeks we would find something archeologists have been unable to discover in years of excavations. No, my main reason for the trip was to discover some validation of the unusual information I had received in my hypnosis sessions, not to find the Hall of Records.

At the time, I still feared that I might be crazy and that the information was wrong and misleading. Therefore, I hoped to find that somewhere else in the world, other than in my own mind, there was something that corroborated the unusual concepts that I had encountered.

Probably the most challenging memory from my past life regressions had been the "Flying Snake," the method by which I'd been transported from Atlantis to Egypt by falling into a snake's mouth.

I knew that throughout the world there are legends of powerful feathered serpents or flying snakes. For example, the cover of John Anthony West's *Serpent in the Sky* shows an Egyptian painting of a man traveling through the sky on the back of an outstretched snake. Based on my experiences, I believe that this image is likely a representation of the Third Root Race or the Atlantean method of instant transportation by snake power.

Especially among the Maya in Mexico there are numerous references to and images of feathered serpents. Ancient Mayan legend has it that Kukulkan or Quetzlcoatl, the god responsible for the creation of the Mayan civilization, arrived from the east and left on a raft made of serpents. This sounded to me like a mythical memory of the Third Root Race method of snake transportation.

In addition, the ancient Maya have also left numerous stone carvings of men in snakes' mouths.
There is no satisfactory scholarly explanation for the ancient Mayan fascination with snakes or why the Maya created so many images of men in snakes' mouths. Since I knew the Cayce readings said that those Atlanteans aware of the impending breakup of their land had fled to safety lands in the Yucatan and Peru, as well as to Egypt, I suspected that this emphasis on men in snakes' mouths was the early humans' memory of the arrival of the Atlanteans. In any case, I wanted to see these carvings. I felt it would make me feel more comfortable with the rest of the information I had received.

John and I first went to Tulum, a breathtakingly beautiful ruin perched on a cliff overlooking the turquoise Caribbean sea. Here we saw a stone carving of a man falling headfirst. Archeologists have named the carving "The Descending God." I wondered if the ancient Mayas had made this carving to illustrate both someone falling into the snake's jaws and also an individual arriving after being catapulted through space.

We also visited Chichen Itza, the site of an unusual Spring Equinox phenomenon in which sunlight falls in such a way that a huge stone snake's body carved along a stairway leading to the top of the main pyramid appears to undulate. Significantly, the snake's mouth is at the *bottom* of the stairway, so that its body transports one to the *top* of the pyramid. It's as if you enter the snake's mouth at the bottom of the pyramid, and the snake's body transports you into space.

At the Mayan ruins in Tulum, the Castillo, a stone fortress, overlooks the beautiful azure Caribbean sea.

In Tulum, the Descending God falls headfirst, with legs spread apart, into an open doorway as if he's falling into the mouth of a snake.

The main pyramid at the Chichen Itza Mayan ruin.

Two serpents with heads at ground level and tails up to the sky flank the stairway of the main pyramid in Chichen Itza, site of the famous Spring Equinox event.

A close up of one of the serpent heads at the bottom of the stairs of the main Chichen Itza pyramid.

John humors me by pretending to be a man with his head in the feathered serpent's mouth.

The steps in Chichen Itza are so steep that many people hold on to a chain to keep their balance. This young mother prefers to sit and wait while her husband climbs.

There are many carvings of snake heads at Chichen Itza.

Although I was impressed with the many carvings of snakes in Chichen Itza, my most important destination in the Yucatan was Uxmal. I had read that according to legend, Uxmal's primary pyramid was constructed overnight by a sorcerer who could fly stones through the air. This sounded like the Atlantean ability to dematerialize and rematerialize stone as I had seen in my hypnosis sessions on the construction of the three Great Pyramids in Egypt.

I had also read in *The World Before* that Ruth Montgomery, who uses automatic writing to receive psychic information from her guides, had said that she believed the Mayan Hall of Records was in Uxmal. The Cayce readings say that it could be uncovered at what would appear to be a sundial that would be to the west of and overshadowed by a temple.

We were pleased to find a sundial in Uxmal in the middle of a courtyard to the west of the site's main temple—the same temple that was the subject of the flying stones legend. On the other side of the sundial were the cubicles of what is called the Nunnery Quadrangle. These small chambers look like the cells of a nuns' cloister. With the sundial to the west of and overshadowed by the temple, the location seemed very much like the place suggested in the Cayce readings.

In February 1999, when John and I had been in Uxmal, archeologists were in the process of exploring inside the oval pyramid. Our guide, a modern Mayan, told us that the ancient Maya built temples on top of temples. Among the guide's people there is a legend that under the oval pyramid is an older flat-sided pyramid. This original flat-sided pyramid was the object of the archeologist's search. The original pyramid under the oval pyramid, and perhaps under the flat-sided pyramid, is the legendary one built of flying stones in one night.

The oval-shaped Pyramid of the Sorcerer dominates the Mayan ruins in Uxmal.

At the Pyramid of the Sorcerer, the sundial is to the left of the stairs, just outside of the photograph.

The image on the left shows the sun dial as it appears from the stairs of the Pyramid of the Sorcerer. The photo on the right shows the sundial from the opposite direction with the stairs of the Pyramid of the Sorcerer behind the sundial.

Here you can see that there is at least one smaller pyramid inside this pyramid.

When I read the plaque describing this pyramid, I was delighted to see that it was called, "The Pyramid of the Goblin." A goblin. What a marvelous way to describe the "frog-like being" that controlled the Crystal in the Atlantean tower. Had I been a goblin?

I remembered that when we had been in Tulum, most of the doorways of the temples had been so low that archeologists had speculated that the ancient builders of these ruins might have been dwarves. How about goblins? Short green-skinned androgynous pixie-faced goblins that could levitate?

Coincidentally, some of the passageways in the Great Pyramid are also less than four feet high.

When we were in Uxmal, I asked the guide if there remained any carvings of a man in a serpent's mouth. Most of these stone carvings have been plundered, many by archeologists who have taken them away for display in museums. The guide told me to look on the back wall of what is called the Nunnery Quadrangle. Here is where I finally found what I was looking for.

Carved in stone on the side of the building, the body of a huge snake undulates along the top of the east-facing wall of the courtyard. The snake faces carvings of the planet Venus as if the snake is flying up into space. Inside its wide-open mouth is the face of a man. It is as if the serpent is flying the man into space.

I would have been satisfied just to have seen and photographed this image of the man's face emerging from the snake's mouth. But there were snake images all over the ruins.

There are many explanations for the ancient Mayan fascination with snakes and especially for their many carvings of men in snake's mouths. These explanations range from snake cults to fertility symbols. However, none of these theories consider that they may represent beings different from ourselves—namely the Third Root Race with their ability to use, via an agreement with nature, the snake's strike capability for propulsion.

An image of a large feathered serpent undulates along the top half of this building in the Nunnery Quadrangle in Uxmal.

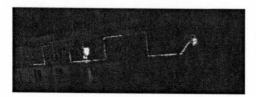

This nighttime image makes it easy to see the whole serpent's body.

To the right of the feathered serpent's face, in the bottom right, there are a number of stylized images of Venus.

People in my seminars have told me that the concentric-square figure to the right of the serpent's head is an infinity symbol.

In this extreme close up, you can see the nose and eyes of the man inside the serpent's mouth. The serpent's face is stylized with a very big upper lip and a large lower jaw.

I have since learned that in Egypt there are also many images of snakes used for transportation. In *The Traveler's Key to Ancient Egypt*, author John Anthony West shows snakes with wings, with feet, in the shapes of boats, and with people riding on their backs. Most of these images are taken from the tombs of Amenhotep II and Thutmoses III in the Valley of the Kings near Luxor. I was especially interested in one snake with a man on its back, flying toward the stars. This image appears in a mural depiction of the Eleventh Hour from The Book of What is in the Duat in the tomb of Thutmoses III.

Based on my memories of Atlantis in past life regressions, I believe that the Yucatan snakes with men in their mouths have feathers because they fly people through the air. In the same way, the serpents in Egypt that are drawn with wings and feet—as well as those that fly to the stars with men on their backs—all represent the same thing: Atlanteans traveling to Egypt and the Yucatan.

However, before I go any further, I want to make it clear that these images, whether in the ruins of the ancient Maya or in the tombs of the Egyptian pharaohs, were not created during the time that the Atlanteans were traveling to Egypt and the Yucatan. They are images created to commemorate a time long ago in the ancient Mayas' and ancient Egyptians' memory.

By way of explanation, we no longer live during the time of Buddha. Nonetheless, many people today have statues of the Buddha in their homes. In the same way, although Jesus the Christ no longer walks the Earth, Christians today adorn the walls of their homes with images of the crucifixion and may wear the crucifix on a metal chain around their necks.

Just because images of Buddha and Christ are still manufactured and used by devotees today, does not mean that either of these holy men are still walking among us now as human beings. They did long ago and we remember them for the great things they did and the wonderful lessons they taught us.

Likewise, I believe that the images in the pharaoh's tombs and in the Mayan ruins are images of an event or events that occurred long before the time of the people who painted the images.

They are images of a time that human beings can hardly comprehend.

As the memories were passed down from generation to generation, the stories became unbelievable because we presently do not experience Light Beings that can disappear and reappear, that can melt with existing animals, and that can wield amazing creative power over the physical.

The Cayce readings say that when Atlantis began to break up, Atlanteans traveled to safety lands in Egypt and Yucatan. I believe that these feathered serpents and winged or footed snakes validate the Cayce readings.

We have been looking for proof of Atlantis without success because we have been looking for evidence of beings like ourselves —human beings. We didn't realize that the documentation was in front of us all along.

Based on my trance memories, I believe we would much better understand the builders of the Great Pyramids, the Pyramid of the Sorcerer, and various other pyramids throughout the world, if we would consider that the builders of these marvels were beings very different from human beings. They were of the Third Root Race— beings capable of a profound power over the physical. They communicated telepathically, levitated, rejuvenated themselves, and cooperated with the natural world to create architectural wonders that even today we cannot reproduce.

When We Were Gods

Wherever there are multi-tonned boulders molded perfectly together, wherever there are myths of the overnight construction of pyramids, wherever legends tell of stones flying through the air, and wherever there are carvings of flying snakes and feathered serpents, there you will find the evidence of the Third Root Race Atlanteans and the time when we were gods.

24

A New World

One cool spring evening John and I stood in our little kitchen preparing hot cups of tea. John leaned against the sink and I against the dishwasher as we waited for the water to boil.

I love John deeply, but it has not been easy for me to talk to him about the information unearthed in the hypnosis sessions. Our minds are in two different worlds. Most of the time I keep all the New Age revelations to myself. But every once in a while, they overflow into our conversations.

"You know," I said, "I supposedly came into the Earth to free you."

"Oh yeah?" he said, giving me that soft, quizzical look he'd had when I first told him I'd dreamt about him. It was a look that said, "What a cute little thing you are with such strange ideas."

"Yeah, that's why I was attracted to you. I was looking for you. You had become entangled in the physical long before we arrived."

He said nothing but reached over my head to get a mug out of the cupboard.

"That's why I saw you as an ape-like being," I continued. "I came to get you free. I was looking for you."

He nodded and pursed his lips, turning the mug in his hands. Then he looked over at our stainless steel kettle, which was starting to make a hissing noise.

"The trouble is," I continued, "I don't know how to get myself out, never mind you, too." I looked up at John. He gave me that soft smile again. I met his eyes.

"No kidding," I said. "Our leader was the being that became the Christ. He led a group of us to free all of you. I was in the expedition. But we got stuck, too. Everyone but the Christ. It was like a whirlpool. That's why He became the first Adam—to make a way out for us."

"You thought that up?" John laughed. "You sure have a good imagination."

"It's not my imagination," I said. "It's from the hypnosis sessions."

He shook his head, but I could see that some part of him was interested. We poured hot water into our mugs and went and sat down in the living room in front of the wood stove. He opened the firebox and poked at the burning logs, stopping to take a tentative sip from his hot mug.

"Yeah, you were lucky to just be an ape-like being," I said. "Some of the Light Beings got really mixed up in animal bodies, with wings and hooves and stuff like that."

"With an imagination like that you should write a book," he said with a chuckle, because he knew I was writing this book. I could tell he was getting bored. I tried to think of a topic from my hypnosis sessions that would interest him.

"Do you know why Einstein and all the scientists after him could not integrate gravitational waves with electromagnetic waves in the Unified Field Theory?" I asked.

He closed the doors of the wood stove and looked at me cautiously.

"It's because they didn't take into account that gravity has a wow to it," I said.

His eyebrows raised slightly.

"You know—a wow, a swell. You know how the ocean has waves on top of the surface of the water? But there's also a swell—a long, deep wave that moves under the smaller surface waves. It's

182

the same with gravity—it also has a swell. That's why gravity is so hard to integrate with electromagnetism."

He turned to me, his eyes flecked with bouncing light. I had his attention!

"That's why we'll need three pyramids—one in Egypt, one in the Yucatan, and one in Atlantis—to still the swell in . . . "

"Atlantis?" he interrupted.

"It's supposed to rise during the upcoming earth changes."

I hesitated, expecting a retort, but he just looked like he had indigestion. So I plowed ahead. "For some reason it's important that all three of the pyramids be surrounded by water. The one in the Yucatan is on a peninsula already. The Atlantean one will be— it literally comes out of the water. And the one in Egypt will have water around it after the upheavals."

He gave me a queer look. "The pyramids in Egypt are in the desert."

"Yeah, I know," I replied, "but after the earth changes, they'll be surrounded by water."

"OK," John said as he shifted toward me in his chair and lifted his mug. "It's conceivable that the Sahara will no longer be desert . . ."

I interrupted. "Do you know that the Gizah plain was once green with vegetation? It looked like a fertile flood plain."

"Yeah, I know."

Now I was the one to be surprised. "Really? How'd you know?"

"Saw it in *National Geographic*, I think. Maybe shuttle pictures or a high-flying jet. Anyway, you could see evidence of a river that used to empty into the Atlantic Ocean, of all things."

"Really!" I opened my mouth and covered it with my hand. It was always shocking to hear a confirmation of the information from the hypnosis sessions.

"Well, the Great Pyramid's going to be surrounded by water again," I said, encouraged. "The whole thing will work when the Great Pyramid gets lined up correctly with some star or star systems. Then once the capstone's on it, the system can function the way it's supposed to."

I looked into John's face to see his reaction. He had grown solemn.

"What bothers me," he said, "is all this talk about the end of the world. The world's not going to end for over a trillium years."

"I agree," I said. "That's the universe though. And then another universe will start up again. It's like the Buddhists say that every world is one breath of God. Each breath lasts trillions and trillions of years. However, that doesn't mean that things here on Earth are going to stay the same all that time. We've got some earth changes coming up, and then we're going to become the Fifth Root Race."

He looked away and sighed. I was losing him fast. He yawned.

I sighed.

He walked over to the sofa, sat down, yawned again and was snoring in 10 seconds.

"Mom," said Clair from the dining room, "tell us more about the Golden Ones.

"It's about kids like us, isn't it?"

I smiled and sat down with my daughters. Miriam, my youngest, was still in high school at the time, and Clair was home for the weekend.

"What I don't get," said Miriam, "is the Fourth Root Race. That's us now, isn't it?"

I nodded in agreement.

"Well, if we were originally Light Beings," she continued, "and then sort of whiffs of smoke and then powerful beings that could move huge stones—and if we're going to be able to appear and disappear in the Fifth Root Race—that means that right now we're the . . . the . . . you know . . . the lowest."

"You're right. That's exactly it. We're at the turning point. The purpose of being tied to these animal-like bodies was to overcome our addiction to the physical. We had to "hit bottom" before we would want to get free again. The problem is our free will. This

Fourth Root Race was supposed to suffer, die, and grieve. It would make us yearn to be free. It's working."

"So the Fourth Root Race was made dense on purpose?

"Yeah. That's why so much of us is evolved from animals. Our bodies are, and to some degree so are our minds and our emotions, but our real self is not. We are Light Beings. In between lifetimes and in our sleep—and in our intuitive hunches and imaginations— we are more like our real selves."

"So reincarnation just belongs to the Fourth Root Race— to humanity?"

"Right. The animal body dies because animals die. It's part of the cycle of the natural kingdom—the seasons, compost, you know . . ."

"OK, you mean the body dies because it's part of the animal world, but our real self doesn't die. It goes into another baby— that's the soul entering at birth, right?"

"Exactly. We say that we have a soul. But I've learned that our soul has us. We are a soul that temporarily has a body. It isn't even that our soul is housed in our body, locked up in there, wanting to get out. It's that because of the way our eyes and brains function, we can't see the Light Being that we really are, which is intermeshed with our physical bodies. Some people can see it—the aura. But most of us see only the physical, the body.

I looked deep into Miriam's eyes.

"When I look at you, I'm looking at a Light Being," I said.

She looked back and smiled.

"OK," she said. "So how's this so different from the Third Root Race—the Atlanteans, the ones who could go in and out of bodies and be in many bodies at once?"

"It isn't—only that now we are enmeshed with only one body— a primate-type of body. We can no longer 'play' with trees or crystals or animals, but we could once."

Clair had been listening quietly while Miriam and I talked. Now she asked, "But if we're more like our real selves when we die and when we sleep, why can't we move all over the universe in between lifetimes like we did before we became stuck in the physical?"

"I've wondered about that, too. I think it's because, although we are no longer in an animal-type body, when we die, we're still caught in the physical just as we were when we were a wisp-of-smoke. You know when those angelic beings healed my body after the torture in the dungeon?"

She nodded.

"Well," I continued, "they were working not on my real body but on something like a blueprint of it. It's this thought form blueprint of a body that is caught here—even in between lives."

I always enjoy talking with my children and also with their friends. For the most part they are open-minded, and they have good ideas. But what I like the best about them is that they are so sincere. And they are so concerned for our world. At a time of life when my generation only cared about "doing our own thing," young people today are intensely involved in causes. Whether it's for the environment or those less fortunate, I see young people while still in grade school, high school, college, and out in the world taking the time to raise money or help those in need. At a time when we were dropping out, many of them are passionately involved.

They are sincere and hard working, and, although occasionally beset with doubts, they manage an abiding optimism. At the age when we raged angrily, they simply and quietly do what they can. Of course there are also many among them who succumb to despair and temporarily lose their way. But isn't this what youth is all about? Didn't Mark Twain say that when he was a young man he was practicing for the gallows?

The media are quick to inform us of every misstep the young make. But on the whole, in spite of occasional confusion, I see a fierce determination in our youth, and I like it.

Many of these young people, and others being born now, truly are the hope of the world. The future is in their hands. It seems plausible to me that this upcoming generation could indeed have a pattern for the future within them that the human race has previously been unable to apply. If nothing else, they certainly have a global awareness. Their view of the Earth is of the whole Earth from space—Spaceship Earth.

Clair broke into my reverie. "OK, Mom, so tell us about the Golden Ones and the Fifth Root Race."

I smiled. "Funny you should mention it. That's just what I was thinking about. Well, you know this is just some far out stuff from my hypnosis sessions . . ."

"Yeah, we know you're up-tight about it," said Clair, while both girls rolled their eyes and looked knowingly at each other. "Just tell us. We'll decide what to do with it."

"OK. It seems that when the Fourth Root Race—you, know, the human race. . ."

"Yeah, yeah . . ."

"Well, when we, the Fourth Root Race, were being created, there was an anticipation of an end of it. The Earth goes through these cyclical upheavals, you know, like the Flood and the Ice Age . . ."

I looked at Clair and Miriam's faces to see if they were following me. Their faces said, "Get on with it."

"OK. Some of us took on different tasks for the time when the Earth would again go through upheavals. It seems I took on . . . "

"Mom," Clair interrupted, "get to the point! We know all this. Tell us about the Golden Ones. How do we know which of us are the ones and what we are to do?"

"It's in the unconscious. Just as the hypnosis unlocked my supposed purpose, the pattern for the new world is in the unconscious of certain young people."

"So we've all got to go for past life regressions?"

"No. Remember, I dreamt about John before I met him. You can access the unconscious through your dreams, your hunches, your gut feelings—you will just know things—and in the things that come to you, by synchronicity. But you've always got to measure everything with your common sense. You have to differentiate between the unconscious impressions from your body, complexes from situations in this lifetime, and karmic patterns from past lifetimes. You wouldn't jump off a bridge if someone told you, would you? Same thing with your unconscious. You always measure your guidance against your common sense. You also must weigh your impressions by whether or not they hurt you or anyone else. The information has to be helpful."

"OK. So you're having trouble saying that the Golden Ones will be the survivors of the earth changes."

I pursed my lips. "Yeah. I don't want to frighten you. It may not happen."

Clair shrugged her shoulders and took a breath as if she was going to argue. I continued before she could say anything. "It's just that prophecy is a funny thing. It's easy to misunderstand. I've told you about that dream I had before you were born?"

"The one with the Chinese holy man who said you'd have a girl next?"

"No, the one I had after you were conceived that said you'd be born in a hospital."

"OK. Yeah. What about it?"

"Well, because I had this dream showing a nurse carrying you through a hospital door, I assumed there was going to be some problem with the birth—that I'd have to go to a hospital instead of have a home birth as I had planned."

"But there wasn't a problem . . ."

"Exactly. It was the exact opposite. The labor was so easy that I thought I was having a false labor, and so I went to the doctor's office. It turned out you were about to come out, and we didn't have time to drive all the way back to the house for a home birth. So you were born in the hospital."

"OK. What does this have to do with the Fifth Root . . .?"

"What I'm trying to say is that it often isn't until afterward that we understand what a prophecy really means. And fear can distort the intent of the prophecy.

"For example, I recently dreamt that each root race experiences time differently. Well, that could explain the Biblical prophecy of the end of time. It could actually mean the end of time 'as we human beings understand it.' Remember, the little frog-being in the Atlantean tower? He didn't know how to measure time like we do. Maybe the Fifth Root Race will understand time differently as well. Therefore, the prophecy may not mean, with a scary interpretation, 'THE END!' but just 'the end of time as we know it.'"

"Wait a minute," said Miriam. "Wait a minute. Are you saying that some day we're only going to be the Fifth Root Race? No more human beings?"

I looked up and said, "I haven't made that obvious?"

"No, Mom, you haven't made that obvious."

"We're supposed to be in a transition during which a new being will emerge.

"When we reincarnate the next time, it may be into this new kind of being."

There was an uncomfortable silence.

Finally Clair spoke as she shrugged her shoulders. "Yeah, OK. I get it."

I heaved a big sigh.

"So that's why you're so up-tight!" said Clair.

"Yeah. And because of the earth changes. But maybe I've got it wrong. Maybe it's just about my own self changing. Maybe it's really about something else. Maybe Bob Frissell is right and droves of aliens surrounding the Earth will protect us from earth changes. Ruth Montgomery says the earth changes have been postponed and that the next president will help people to relocate to safety lands. I've also read that the earth changes might be very gradual. One woman has seen psychic impressions of the new world. It's called the 'I Am America Map'." There's also speculation that the population will be reduced by infertility. In other words, the earth changes will be in the 'earth' of the physical body. Often prophecy is just a warning that says . . ."

"Mom!" said Clair, "it's OK. Enough. We can handle it. We're handling the ozone hole, greenhouse gases, AIDS, nuclear proliferation, pollution, Chernobyl, the destruction of the wilderness, acid rain, genocide..." Her dark blue eyes looked deeply into mine. "For God's sake," Clair gave me her famous stare, "we can handle cyclical earth upheavals."

I sucked in my breath. "I believe you."

My children. My babies. How could we have given them a world so lacking in hope? I had spent my whole adult life nurturing, caring for, and loving them. All I wanted for them was a rosy future, but there was hardly even a future for them to contemplate.

What if my vision was real? What if all the evil that swirled around them really did just fall away, giving them a whole new world to start with?

In my research I'd found so many books that seemed to corroborate the information in the hypnosis sessions. The concept of the root races and many different worlds was not new. It was actually very old. What if there was really something to it?

The Hopi Nation in Northeastern Arizona said that the Creator had destroyed three worlds before our present one and that we were on the brink of the destruction of the fourth because we refused to change our ways. They had even gone to the United Nations to warn the world of this impending "purification." The Hopi believed that disaster could be averted if we returned to an appreciation of the Earth and nature.

The Hindus believe in previous worlds. They feel that in our present Fourth World Age, our spiritual dignity is gone and so only ruthlessness prevails.

There were also the Maya, who expected the new world to begin December 23, 2011. (I had said it would not begin until after 2011.) And Cayce, Madame Blavatsky, and the Austria clairvoyant whose wisdom underlies the Waldorf Schools, Rudolf Steiner, also referred to the root races.

"Mom," Clair broke through my thoughts. I looked up. Her face was flushed. "Mom, we need a future—even if it is weird. Tell us about the Golden Ones."

Of course they needed a future—and I had seen one.

Clair tried to get me started.

"OK. So now the Earth is a mess, the earth changes are over ..."

She stopped and frowned as if she had just thought of something. "Wait a minute. How do we know if it's the earth changes or just a regular hurricane or earthquake or tornado or volcano? You know, the Earth does this stuff all the time."

I nodded. "You'll know, believe me. When it's happening, some parts of the world might have daylight for longer than a day. Those parts that are experiencing night will have an extra-long night. The sun will appear to move in the sky. When it's all over, the sun will probably rise and set in a different part of the sky."

Clair and Miriam looked at each other. "Cool," they said at the same time and then turned to me, their eyes shining.

"OK," said Clair, "the earth changes are over, nature is recovering, and the Golden Ones have survived. They're going to reactivate the Great Pyramid?"

"Either they are or their children, the Fifth Root Race," I said.

"What then? Surprise me."

'OK, the Immaculate Conception. Remember, the Christ is supposed to show us the way out."

"Cool. So we're just going to get pregnant."

"Maybe. I really don't know. It seems like it. It makes sense. But I don't really know. That's for you to find out. It's my main purpose just to say, 'This is it. This is the time that you are here for. Awaken!' And to remind you who you really are, what you're really doing here, and where you're really going. The only thing I saw was babies that disappeared when their mothers were holding them."

"And then the babies reappeared again?" asked Clair.

"Right."

"That's the Fifth Root Race?"

"Right. They'll probably communicate telepathically. They're beings that aren't as tightly held by the physical as we are."

"Cool. And they looked like normal babies?"

"Actually they seemed to have larger heads and larger, puffier eyes. Maybe smaller legs."

"And will we nurse them?"

"Probably. But I don't really know. I said the Fifth Root Race could rejuvenate like the Third Root Race. You know, the power beings—the gods and goddesses."

"So what's so different about the Fifth Root Race compared to the gods and goddesses?"

"Their will. The Fifth Root Race will want to be free—to go home. They won't have rebellion. They'll live love. Remember, Satan will be bound. They won't make war because they are peaceful. When they are challenged, their first thought won't be to fight. They'll have different reactions than we do. They won't destroy nature like we do because they won't be afraid. They will know how to cooperate with nature like the power beings, but they won't wallow in the physical or create fantastic things that say how great they are. Their first purpose will be to help each other."

"I'd like that," said Clair.

"Me, too," said Miriam.

"Me, too," said I.

"Me, too," mumbled John from the living room. He must have been snoring and listening at the same time—truly a genius at the sofa. I walked over to the couch and sat down beside him. He was stretched out with his long legs crossed on the coffee table, his head flopped back against a pillow.

Without opening his eyes or closing his mouth, he reached his arm behind me and pulled me close. I snuggled up to him.

You never know what's going to happen when you find the man of your dreams.

25

Going Home

Our unconscious contains memories of who we really are. That's why we're so entranced by space stories, UFOs, aliens, The Force, etc. The memories are in the imaginative mind whether they're accessed through the pineal—intuition and the psychic—or the pituitary—imagination.

If we are fascinated with the pyramids or the Maya, we were probably there. If science and technology enthralls us, we were probably in Atlantis.

Our longing for transcendence of the physical is another indication that we, in our essence, are something different from a modified animal form. We won't eat meat, denying that we are part of the animal world that lives by killing its food, or we try to be as thin as possible, trying to negate that we have a body at all, or we clothe our bodies in diaphanous fabrics or make our homes palaces, our vehicles spaceships, our churches cathedrals. All this is from yearning, yearning, yearning for what we once were and what we long to be again—pure Light that is one with the Creator.

Although, to the animal-type beings we now find ourselves, the idea of being pure Light appears to be absurd, we are haunted by feelings of longing. Our religions help us to cope with this very real feeling that we are far from home and lonely. Through our religions we do our best to explain our feeling of incompleteness.

We say we are lost. And so, although being pure Light seems absurd to us, we long for the type of melting experience we could only know in the vibrational state. Our yearning to fall in love, to immerse ourselves in causes, to create empires, to possess, to be drunk or stoned are all attempts to fill this loneliness.

We long again to travel instantaneously by thought and melt into everything, understanding our world through pure vibration. We yearn for enlightenment, to see the Light, to be one with the Light. Although we don't want to think that we are actually Light Beings, our language betrays us. How else can we be one with the Light unless we are Light itself?

It is absolutely ridiculous to want to live in a body forever. If it was our rightful goal, would not Christ, by His example, have shown us how to live in a body forever?

The resurrection is not about being in the physical forever but about returning to our Light-Being form. At the end of the Gospel of Luke when the Christ ascended, He had His hands up—in the "God is Greater" pose—and He dematerialized, shimmered, disappeared.

There is a popular conception today that we have to struggle very hard to be good enough for God. That we're never quite there. That only certain special ones—denoted by church if we're religious, denoted by wealth if we're materialistic, denoted by followers if we seek fame, denoted by conquests if we love power, denoted by people helped if we're motivated by altruism—deserve to progress, as if it's some kind of a contest. It isn't. We are all right now who we need to be. We always have been. We always will be. The Light Being that you really are still is. And it loves you with all your heart.

When we are entreated in religious texts to love our neighbors as ourselves or to do no harm, it isn't so much that we must do these things to be good enough. It is because by doing so, we more closely align with our real selves. When we love God with all our heart and mind and soul and our neighbor as ourselves, when our intention is to help humanity, when we are able to love even those who despicably use us, we resonate more closely with our souls, we feel at peace—and we come closer to who we really are and our true destiny.

You don't have to go up to the highest mountain or down to the deepest sea. It is here with you all the time. And so it is with everyone. It is only that you have been taught and that your eyes do not see the glow of the Light Being you are.

Who we really are feels like our heart, because who we really are is a heart that shines with a Light so bright that it fires the universe.

And whether we like it or not, it is inevitable that we will remember who we really are and return to our true nature.

It matters not whether we die today or tomorrow. We will always be and have always been.

We have been looking for God in all the wrong places, because God is within us. All we have to do is to remember.

Let me tell you a story about a darling little boy I used to know. When he was about six years old, we would often go swimming together. But he would only splash about because he didn't really know how to swim. I told him that swimming was really easy because the water automatically held you up and made you float. He said that it didn't. That's why he had to splash so much—to try to keep himself up.

I told him that he had to put his face in the water. If he did, he would find out that the water automatically would hold him up and he would float. I showed him how to do it, taking a breath and stretching myself over the water as if I was lying on it. He saw how I floated.

"Now," I said, "you do it."

And he did. He took a breath, held it, put his face in and stretched out over the water. He took an amazing risk by setting aside his preconceived ideas based on his real experience of sinking. And of course he floated. The look of triumph on his face when he stood up was marvelous. The memory of it still warms my heart.

"I did it!" he exclaimed. "It's easy!"

And then he tried it a number of times again. Each time it still worked. He was delighted.

"See, you've just learned how to swim," I told him.

"Oh no," he said, "I knew all along. I had just forgotten."

It's like that with us. We know. We've known all along. It's deep in the heart of us. We've been splashing around trying ever so hard to keep afloat, trying to get good enough, trying to accumulate enough to be worthwhile, trying to be beautiful enough, liked enough, etc. But we don't float. There's something missing. And that something is that we have to put our faces in the water—the water of the unconscious. And then we'll find it's easy. It's there in the unconscious. We've known all along who we really are and where we are really going.

Each of us has our place in the drama that is about to unfold. With all our hearts we thank this world, this planet, this Earth for all it has done for us. We were strangers in this beautiful land. We ask the Earth's forgiveness for any harm we may have done while playing with our energies. We apologize for our naiveté for thinking we are greater than the sunrise or a tree.

We are poised on the brink of our return to our Maker. Whether we will leave with the Son, whether we will remain to birth or be birthed as the new root race, we know the upcoming step will bring us closer to our true destiny.

It seems that we are preparing for a new world.

Humanity, which appears to be bound by the physical, is meant to fly with the gods. Mother Earth is about to birth a new world. The difficulties, confusions, trials, and fears of our times are the throes of her labor.

It will help you as it has helped me, to look to your unconscious where dwells the God within, because there you will find who you really are, what you are really doing here and where you are really going. Whatever you need at this time will be there for you.

Remember, when you look in the mirror, you are looking at a Light Being. When you look at your partner, your children, your parents, those you contact in your everyday life, you are interacting with Light Beings.

Whatever your role may be in the upcoming emergence of this new world, remember, you are Light, you are Love, you are eternal and you are going home.

May God bless you and keep you forever.

Part II:

Articles

26

Introduction to the Articles

The following are a collection of published articles I've written concerning similar topics as covered in the book. Although some of the information in the articles is also in the book, each article also contains unique information.

For example, the two articles published in *Venture Inward*, the membership magazine of Edgar Cayce's Association for Research and Enlightenment (A.R.E.), contain references to specific Cayce psychic readings, as does "The Great Crystal," published in *Circle* magazine.

"Melting Off the Pounds," provides a list of benefits derived from pursuing the morning sunlight exercises. The *Fate* article, "Arcturus is Home," further describes the relationship between Orion, Arcturus, and the Sphinx. In "The Man of My Dreams," I explain how I work with my dreams to bring guidance into my life. Finally, the *Alternate Perceptions* article, "In the Mouth of the Snake," describes my experiences in Egypt looking for images of winged serpents and further validation of my Atlantis memories.

27

From Obesity to the Fifth Root Race

Originally appeared in
Venture Inward
Nov./Dec. 1998, Volume 14 Number 6
www.edgarcayce.org/venture_inward

All I wanted was to lose weight. So, I went to a hypnotherapist. In the hypnosis, I was shown a scene that represented my purpose in life. It was to prepare the survivors of the upcoming upheavals. They would bring in a new type of being, the Fifth Root Race.

Whew, I thought, when I came out of the hypnosis, I am reading too much Cayce.

Not necessarily, my hypnotherapist told me. It was also possible that I was experiencing something real. After all, many of us who are drawn to the Cayce readings are likely part of a group incarnating together. Since Edgar Cayce had referred to the Fifth Root Race in his readings, there was a chance that my unconscious knew about it also.

But what does the Fifth Root Race have to do with my obesity, I wondered?

My first hypnosis session was in October 1995. I had just had a miscarriage. Although I had had a weight problem most of my life—yo-yoing 20 or 30 pounds for years—I had never before experienced such a relentless weight gain as I had suffered after the miscarriage.

The doctors called it a hormonal imbalance. I called it a disaster. In four months, I had gained 50 pounds. Every two or three weeks, I had to buy clothes of a larger size. At times, I was gaining a pound a day. I wondered if soon I would have trouble fitting into a theater seat or squeezing through the bathroom door.

I went to four doctors. They all took thyroid tests but the results were normal. One doctor said that hormonal imbalances were not unusual with very young and very old mothers. I was 47, the mother of three older children from a previous marriage.

Hypnotherapy seemed like my last resort. I was especially discouraged because, just before the pregnancy, I had finally learned how to control my weight by using suggestions in the Cayce readings: diet, exercise, colonics, osteopathic adjustments, fume baths, massages, and the radio-active or impedance device. For the first time in my life, I had not only lost weight but I had kept it off—and lost another five pounds during the year that I maintained the loss. But after my miscarriage, it was like an obesity switch had been turned on.

I knew that hypnosis had helped Edgar Cayce when he lost his voice. I had also read in *Many Mansions* that the Cayce readings had attributed problems of an endocrine nature to experiences in past lives. Maybe a past-life regression could clarify the cause of my sudden weight gain.

In reading 1339-1, a 17-year-old obese girl was diagnosed with incoordination of the glands. Her life reading said that she had been an Olympic-level athlete in ancient Greece and Rome. She "excelled in beauty, in the ability to carry in figure, in body, the games that were a part of the experience." However, "too oft did the entity laugh at those less nimble of activity, owing to their heaviness in body." (1339-2) In this lifetime, she was "meeting same" by being overweight and having to work out her karma by diet and outdoor exercise.

Was my obesity the result of mockery in a previous lifetime? If so, I was ready to face it now. Anything, rather than win the Guinness world record for the fastest weight gain in history.

My therapist said that it often helped, with such problems, to go to the "karmic causative factor," which might be in this or a past life. A child called "Piggie" as a normal plump toddler might, for example, grow up to become an obese adult because unconsciously she believes she really is a "Piggie."

In our early sessions we were unable to establish a causative factor in this life. In a later session, I found myself at the mouth of a cave. It was nighttime. Stars shone over dark vegetation outside the cave. Emotions can be amazingly intense during a past-life regression, and I was feeling utterly and desolately lonely.

"I want to go home," I sobbed.

"Where is home?" asked the therapist.

"Arcturus."

I told her that I could get home through a lighted place on the hill. At first it looked like a flying saucer, but then I realized it was a swirling vortex of clouds—a Star Gate out of our solar system.

Interestingly, I later found this statement in reading 5755-2: "There are centers through which those of one solar system may pass to another . . ."

When my therapist asked me to further describe my situation, I replied, "It's somehow different. It doesn't seem as if I am as solid as I am (today) . . . it's like I'm translucent or something." Suddenly I began to cry and wail, "It's about being stuck! I can sort of glide, but I can't get free!"

Cayce also describes the "entanglement" of a soul in the physical.

I was like a genie who hovered over a lamp. A translucent swirl of smoke, I could get out of the "lamp," but I couldn't get free. My therapist suggested that we discover how I came to be entangled and asked that I go back to the time when I could easily get home. To my surprise, I found myself pure light—a light beam. Without a physical body, my experience of the Earth was entirely by vibration. I danced on undulating waves of color accompanied by sounds, like music, that coincided with the various vibrations.

My mission from God was to explore His creations. I was part of a group looking for companions who had become entangled in the physical. As I searched deeper, I began mingling with the vibrations rather than only dancing on them. I delved into a vibration so deep and bone-rattling that it was like the deepest tones of a gigantic pipe organ. The waves of vibration were no longer bright colors of pink, blue, and purple. Everything became a dull orange-brown haze. Down below me, there was an ape-like beast. This was the being I had been seeking.

However, I, too, became entangled. When the therapist asked what I was doing, I said that I was playing. When she asked me what type of play, I reluctantly answered, "Well, it's sexual."

No longer a light beam, I was now the translucent being I had first seen in the cave. Like a small cloud, I caressed over and under this apelike being, flitting all around him, enjoying the deep feelings vibrating through both of us. I moved like a wind over his back, between his legs, and along his arms and buttocks.

When I came out of the hypnosis, my therapist and I looked at each other. "Sounds like the sons of God were tempted by the daughters of men," she said. Genesis 6:2 says that "the sons of God saw the daughters of men that they were fair; and they took them wives of all which they chose."

I thought it also sounded like the Fall. I had been tempted and had succumbed. Instead of experiencing past lives, I seemed to have gone even further back in time to "the beginning." As reading 815-7 says, "It was the eating, the partaking, of knowledge; knowledge without wisdom—or that as might bring pleasure, satisfaction, gratifying—not of the soul . . . as of eating of the tree of knowledge."

But what did this have to do with my being overweight and my hormonal imbalance? It appeared as if the karmic causative factor behind my obesity was the Fall. It was as if the overweight condition was a constant reminder to me that I was not free. Just as entanglement in the physical kept me from freely moving through the universe, my weight kept me from freely moving in my present life.

In the same way, all of our infirmities are a constant reminder to us how much we are controlled and confined by our entanglement in the physical.

Obesity also kept me searching. If I hadn't been so miserable, I would never have gone for hypnotherapy. I would have missed learning more deeply about who I really am—a Light Being.

I began to like myself, even though I was obese. I no longer felt that my added weight was a cruel and evil punishment for something I had done in a past life. It was more of an opportunity to seek and learn. Hadn't it brought me to the Cayce readings and the hypnotherapist?

I was also curious about this first lifetime. Was it sex with the ape-like being that had caused the Fall, or was it something else? We decided to go back to the time when I had changed from pure light to a translucent wisp-of-smoke, searching for what exactly had caused my fall into the physical.

In the hypnosis, I came to the time when I was just about to enjoy the vibrations with the beast. My therapist told me to ask my unconscious mind what I could learn from being at this crucial place of change. I replied that just at the moment when I wanted to mix my vibrations with the apelike beast, I had split the quality of humility from me. It had floated away, but still hovered nearby. By separating myself from humility, I had separated myself from God.

So that's what had caused the Fall. I wanted not only to explore, but to experience. To do that, I had separated myself from humility that kept me within God's will.

It wasn't the sex. True, the desire to experience sexual vibrations had tempted me to split off the humility. But, it wasn't the sex per se. It was disobedience—the original sin.

While hypnotized, I was led through an exercise in which I was reunited with the humility I had split off.

"And, concerning that desire eventually to go home," asked the therapist, "what do you know in this (united) body about going 'home'?"

"It's inevitable," I replied.

Since that session, I have become much more comfortable with my body and myself. I also care less what people think of me. Before this session, without the humility, I wanted everyone to think I was wonderful. I feared making mistakes, always trying to look good and covering up my failings, as if being alive isn't full of disappointments and frustrations.

Nonetheless, although I better understood the underlying cause of my obesity, I did not yet know how I was going to lose weight. I only knew that I was suffering from a soul sickness called "lack of humility." Although I appeared to be making some progress toward understanding the ailment, I wondered if I would ever find a cure. It seemed beyond me. I was also told that just about everyone suffered with the same disease. We lived our lives as if we were greater than God. We all had our own personal ways of manifesting the problem—in my case, obesity—but, in effect, the reason why we did not align perfectly with our pure light selves was that we believed we had the right to follow our own wills rather than God's.

So, in search of a cure, the hypnotherapy continued. In one session, I was led to a special sanctuary where I could meet those of the Most High who were my "elders, my guardian angels, my companions." They told me the purpose of my present lifetime. We met in a luminous room at the summit of a white mountain at the top of the world. The Christ lovingly led me to an opening in the chamber through which I could see my life. First, I saw upheavals. And then, I was told that my purpose in this lifetime was to "awaken" the survivors of the earth changes to their destiny. They were the Golden Ones who would bring in the Fifth Root Race.

By way of explanation, I was shown a lifetime in Atlantis when I was a being that could go in and out of bodies. One of the bodies I used was a frog. When my therapist asked me whether the frog-being was male or female, I replied that the question didn't apply—

I was androgynous. I used the frog-being's body to control the Great Crystal, the Atlantean power source, in a round room at the top of a tall tower.

"I have the feeling I'm not quite the same kind of person I am now," I said and began to levitate.

When Atlantis began to crumble, I was in a group of oversouls that instantly transported themselves to safety in Egypt. Our purpose was to preserve Atlantean knowledge in the Great Pyramid. At the construction site, I saw Ra, who had been one of Cayce's previous incarnations. He, too, could go in and out of bodies. I saw him in his made-of-gold eagle form, swooping low over the pyramid, literally watching construction with a hawk's eye.

"And what is the reason for your needing to reconnect with this old, old memory now?" asked the therapist.

"My sense is to gather the faithful," I replied. "They have an aligned purpose. They're really sincere people."

These were the Golden Ones, souls who were chosen during the time that Atlantis was breaking up and the Great Pyramid was being built. The Golden Ones had returned, reincarnated at the end of the 20th century. I was to inform them of their destiny to birth the Fifth Root Race and their place in the history of the soul on Earth.

It is one thing to relive these memories while hypnotized, but another thing to come out of the trance and face what you've experienced. It made my head spin. It was outrageous. What was all this mumbo-jumbo about wisps of smoke wafting over ape-like beings and frogs controlling the Great Crystal in Atlantis? I soon realized that instead of reliving past lives, I had been reliving past root races! It was the history of the soul on Earth. As the Bible says, we had originally been created in the image of God. At one time, we were pure light, capable of traversing the universe. But when we "fell" into our entanglement in the physical, we were not immediately the animal-like human beings we presently find ourselves.

We had fallen through a number of different types of beings. First, we had been light beams, the First Root Race. Then, after the Fall, we had become translucent wisps-of-smoke, the Second Root Race. The Third Root Race was an androgynous being that could levitate, go in and out of bodies, and immediately transport itself from Atlantis to Egypt. Our present form, the animal-like human race, was the Fourth Root Race.

The Cayce readings make several references to root races. To a husband and wife who wanted to become self-sufficient through farming, Cayce said in 470-35 that we all should be self-sufficient: "You expect a new race. What are you doing to prepare for it? You must prepare food for their bodies as well as their minds and their spiritual development!"

Two other references to the root races are in reading 5748-6 in which Cayce says that the record of our experiences built into the passages of the Great Pyramid are the history of our present (Fourth) Root Race. This reading also contains an enigmatic reference to the record house to be found beneath the right forepaw of the Sphinx: "This may not be entered without an understanding, for those that were left as guards may *not* be passed until after a period of their regeneration in the Mount, or the Fifth Root Race begins."

Eager to find anything that would help me feel more comfortable with the root-race concept, I discovered a 1994 *Venture Inward* article entitled "The Fifth Root Race" by Kirk Nelson, who had studied the Cayce readings on prophecy. No one thought to ask Mr. Cayce what the four previous root races were, Mr. Nelson writes. However, after studying the Cayce readings for 20 years, he concluded that the four root races were "spirit, thought form, projection into matter, and finally Adamic man or *Homo sapiens*."

These were very similar to the pure light, translucent cloud, ability to go in and out of bodies, and animal-form human beings I had found in my hypnosis sessions. It was heartening to see that someone was writing about the root races. I also discovered volumes of work by the mystic, Madame Helene Blavatsky, who described the root races in great detail.

I wondered if perhaps I had read Mr. Nelson's article in 1994, before my first hypnosis session, and had merely embellished the information with an overactive imagination. However, he could only speculate on what to expect of the upcoming Fifth Root Race, while my hypnosis session had been very specific in revealing that the Fifth Root Race would be born to the survivors of the upcoming earth changes. I called these survivors the Golden Ones. They were young people who were among us now. The Fifth Root Race, the babies born to the Golden Ones, would glow with a golden aura. Unlike ourselves, who muddy our auras with negative thoughts and emotions, they would live in love, keeping their auras always golden. They would be less tied to the Earth, having the ability, even while babies, to disappear and appear again. They also seemed to have a different appearance than we do, having larger heads, more bulging eyes, and shorter legs. They would know who they were (Light Beings) and where they were really going (back to oneness with God). They would not die, but would bring in the thousand years of peace on Earth while Satan slept.

What did this have to do with my overweight? Right after the session in which I'd been told to prepare for the Fifth Root Race, I stopped gaining weight. It was as if the obesity had fulfilled its objective—to bring me to my purpose in life.

In that session, I'd been told to inform the world with this information. I decided to write a book about my experiences. Then, some strange things began to happen in my life—even when I wasn't hypnotized. One night I received a visit from Pan, Lord of the Wilderness. He wanted to be included in the book and gave me suggestions for prayers and activities anyone could do to save the Earth—suggestions which worked on the Biblical principle that 10 good people could save a city. Apparently, the natural world was poised to work with us.

I feared I must be going crazy. I had started out as a minor Cayce "flake," imagining that I knew about the Fifth Root Race, and had graduated to a full-blown "flake," believing that other-worldly beings were trying to contact me.

During this time, I received solace from reading *The Lost Memoirs of Edgar Cayce*, in which Cayce struggles with his own fears of insanity and comes to terms with the information in his trance readings. As far as the earth changes, Cayce, while awake and conscious, writes, "Portions of the Earth are going to be wiped away in the next few years, I feel very sure of that."

It made me feel that there might be some validity to the information in my hypnosis sessions. Nonetheless, I was no Edgar Cayce. I was just a fat mother of three who had had a miscarriage. For eight months I immersed myself in comforting, humdrum, mundane activities, all the while inwardly fretting over the information that had come to me.

Then, I had a dream in which I saw the survivors of the upheavals. They were cold, frightened, alone, and bewildered. In the end, I decided that I could write about my experiences without personally believing in them. There might be a grain of truth in the information. Someone, somewhere, sometime, might benefit from it. So, I went back to writing the book. However, whenever I tried to write about Atlantis, I got stuck. I went for another hypnosis session to get some clarification.

To my surprise, I found myself on trial. The archangels Michael and Gabriel were trying me for pride. Telepathically they told me that pride was jeopardizing my ability to write about Atlantis. I had to admit that I had been daydreaming about becoming rich and famous should the book sell. During the trial, the Christ was my advocate. He knew how difficult it was to be in the flesh. The archangels, who have never become entangled in the physical, were rather harsh and rigid. They had no understanding why I worried about my weight or what people thought of me—such fleeting concerns that changed from lifetime to lifetime. They reminded me that I have lived so many lives before—and had been forever and would continue eternally.

In the end, a compromise was reached. Since it was so important that I share the information, I would not lose any weight until I completed the book. So I wrote a book called *When We Were Gods*.

Since finishing the book, I have made great progress in my original objective—I've lost 26 pounds. It hasn't been easy. I alternate between pridefully imagining that I'll look like a movie star when I'm thin and being pathetically self-pitying about why I can't be like other people who don't have to watch what they eat or exercise religiously. At these times, I stop losing weight and even gain some. There's usually a physical reason for gaining weight, like being undisciplined about the amount of food I'm eating or not taking time to exercise. But the reason is usually my pride.

However, when I sincerely want to have the best body I can, as a reflection of the pure aligned Light Being I know my real self to be, I lose weight easily and quickly. Then, I am thankful that God is mindful of me and is metabolizing the fat out of my body.

And I am very, very grateful.

28

Melting Off the Pounds: The Sun Diet

Originally appeared in
Whole Life Times:
Journal of Holistic Lifestyle
June 1999, Issue 206
www.wholelifetimes.com

Carole Chapman was scared. Every morning when she stepped on the scales, she was a pound heavier. The four doctors she consulted all said the same thing: she had a hormonal imbalance, it was not unusual following a miscarriage and there was nothing they could do for her.

"I didn't know what to do," says the 5'3" tall mother of three. "I'd had trouble with weight my whole adult life, but nothing like this. My attempts at diet and exercise weren't working. At the rate I was gaining, soon I'd have trouble fitting into a theater seat."

A friend suggested she visit a hypnotherapist to tell her body she was no longer pregnant. Unfortunately, when the hypnotherapist used conventional suggestions—that her body return to normal function—there were no positive results. The pounds continued to pile on.

The therapist decided to ask Carole, under hypnosis, what she needed to do to heal her hormonal imbalance. Evidently, the Marquis de Puysegur, who discovered hypnosis in 1784, had found that ordinary people, while in a hypnotic trance, could correctly make medical diagnoses and know things they had never encountered in their ordinary lives.

While under trance, Carole replied that the problem was at the pineal, the pea-sized master gland above and behind the eyes. She said the pineal required natural, unfiltered sunlight to functions properly. Therefore, she was to go outdoors everyday, rain or shine, for at least a half-hour, and she was not to wear glasses or contacts because the light that reached the pineal entered through the eyes. (Taking her glasses off in the house or car didn't count because glass and most plastics filter sunlight, rendering parts of the spectrum missing or out of balance.) According to the information in her hypnosis, the best times for her sun therapy were at around 10 a.m. in the summertime and noon in the winter, probably because ultra-violet is not harmful at those times.

"I have to admit," says Carole, "that at first it was kind of scary to go out into my myopic blur. But I can read without my glasses, so I'd sit in the shade with a book. After awhile, I found I could also putter around the garden. Before long, I was going for walks."

Light therapy is not new. According to Dr. Jacob Liberman, O.D., Ph.D., author of *Light: Medicine of the Future*, (Bear & Co., 1992), the ancient Egyptians built intricate temples of light for healing, and the Greeks believed that light coming in through the eyes could cure internal organs. More recently, blue light has been used in hospitals since the early 1950s to cure jaundice in premature infants. At the present time, research into the healing power of light is being conducted in such diverse fields as cancer, sexual dysfunction, and learning disorders.

Interestingly, although there is little information on the effect of natural unfiltered sunlight on weight loss in humans, farmers have noticed that animals gain weight faster if confined indoors.

To get a fatter animal faster, keep it indoors and under artificial lights.

While hypnotized, Carole said that the problem lay at the pineal. Recent scientific breakthroughs have shown that the pineal, which only a few decades ago was considered vestigial like the appendix, secretes the much-touted hormone melatonin now known to influence, among many other things, reproduction, life span, and immunity.

Probably because the pineal is influenced by the light/dark cycle of the day, Carole was also given an unusual adjunct to her sun therapy.

"The strangest part of the instructions given me in my hypnosis sessions," says Carole, "was that I was to greet the sun as it rose every morning. I was to raise my arms three times and say, 'God is greater.'"

She was told that just about everyone in the modern world suffers with the same soul sickness: Because we live in artificially lighted environments, out of rhythm with the sun, our lifestyles declare that we are greater than God and therefore puts us out of alignment with our souls.

The pineal, also called the third eye, is the site of one of the charkas, where the soul connects with the body. Since this gland contains light-sensitive cells similar to the retina in the eye, it could be that the pineal works best with natural light in the same way that our digestive system works best when we eat foods grown naturally.

Desperate for anything that would help her, Carole made a major change in lifestyle and began to awaken before the dawn. "I won't pretend that it was easy," she says, "but after awhile, I really began to love the sunrise. It's the only time that you see the world go from dark to light. Most of us only see the sunset, when the world goes from light to dark."

Liberman says that the natural light at sunrise resonates higher in the reds, oranges, and yellows of the spectrum, while the sunset is more indigo, blue, and violet. Could it be that Carole, in the same way that some people need more of certain vitamins, required more of the reds and yellows found at sunrise for her pineal to function optimally?

"I can't say that it was the actual sun therapy or that it was because I started to walk in the morning. Eventually, I also ate more healthfully, so maybe it all works together. In any case, at last my weight evened out and, slowly, the pounds started coming off.

"One morning when I was doing the sun greeting, I realized that since we are all supposed to be light in our essence, when I watched the sun rise, I was looking at my self—fat or thin. I realized that compared to the sun and God, all of us are equally tiny. Therefore, I was no less a being than a model or ballerina. This realization has been very freeing for me."

To her delight, Carole's sun therapy helped to heal not only her body, but also her spirit.

---

8 Ways Sun Therapy Can Add to Your Healing Regime

1. Develops a daily routine.
2. Coordinates internal hormonal systems with natural rhythms
3. Raises self-esteem by giving you something you have the power to do. Maybe you can't yet give up chocolate because the habit is so loaded with emotional gratification. In comparison, 30 minutes outside without corrective lenses is easy.
4. Eliminates the destructive and very prevalent attitude that an overweight person is a lesser human being. Under the sun and in God's eyes, you are no less than any other human being on Earth, whatever your size.
5. Reminds you that the Higher Power of the Universe is greater than you and therefore, no matter how much you diet, exercise, get massages, etc., in the end you will have to wait for the spirit in your body to heal you.
6. Starts your day with a positive, joyful outlook, celebrating, at cell level, that the light overcomes the darkness.
7. Reminds you that you are, in essence, Light.
8. Rewards you daily with the most glorious light show on Earth.

WARNING: NEVER LOOK DIRECTLY AT THE SUN! It could cause blindness.

29

Arcturus is Home

Originally appeared in
*FATE: True Reports of the
Strange & Unknown*
July 1999, Volume 52 Number 7
www.fatemag.com

We came to Earth through a Star Gate that looked like a swirling vortex of clouds from this side. The gate functioned like a door between worlds. Our purpose was to explore the universe. Home was Arcturus.

I had gone to a hypnotherapist for help with a sudden weight gain after a miscarriage. To my surprise, when the therapist regressed me to find the "karmic causative factor" behind my weight gain, I experienced my first lifetime on Earth—and I wasn't even human.

At first I couldn't understand what I was perceiving. Expecting to encounter an incarnation from the historical past, I hesitated when the therapist asked me to describe my surroundings.

"It's somehow different," I said. "It doesn't seem as if I'm as solid as I am [now]." There was a long pause and then suddenly I began to cry pitifully, "It's about being stuck!" I wailed. "I'm so sad! Getting stuck!" I sobbed and sobbed remembering the sorrow and terror. "I can sort of glide but I can't get free."

I was translucent—like a wisp-of-smoke—and lived in a cave. It was night outside and I could see stars shinning over dark vegetation. On a distant hill I saw what at first appeared to be a flying saucer. On closer inspection, I realized it was a swirling vortex of clouds lit up in the night sky. I called it a Star Gate.

"I want to go home," I wailed. The therapist asked me where home was. I replied, "Arcturus." But I couldn't go home. Something had happened that made it impossible for me to travel back through the Star Gate.

Curious, the therapist told me to go back to the time when I could still travel through the gate. To my surprise, I found myself pure light—a line of light in three parts—I suppose because Earth is a three-dimensional world. As light, my experience of the Earth was entirely by vibrations. I danced on waves of undulating light, accompanied by ethereal music that coincided with the different wave colors.

I delved into vibrations that were orange-brown in color and sounded like the deepest tones of a great pipe organ. There, I saw the dark form of an ape-like being. I wanted to play with the beast.

"What do you do to play?" asked the therapist.

"Well, it's sexual," I replied. No longer a light beam, I had become a small cloud that caressed over and under and around this black form in the shape of an ape. Like a wind, I brushed over his back, between his legs, and along his arms and buttocks.

"And then what happens?"

I sighed, "Then comes being in the cave [and being stuck]." Evidently I could not traverse the Star Gate until I was again pure light, immortal and free to roam the universe.

When I came out of hypnosis, I had trouble believing what I had experienced. I'm a pretty open-minded person, but I had never expected to discover that I was an alien. The star Arcturus is a yellow-orange giant located 37 light years away from the Earth's solar system. It is one of the closest of the bright stars.

As the hypnosis sessions continued, I explored my life as an alien trapped on Earth. I saw myself transform into a being that could move in and out of animal bodies in Atlantis. When earthquakes began to destroy Atlantis, I was one of a handful of entities that instantly transported ourselves to the safe lands in Egypt where we helped build the three great pyramids.

Since my hypnosis sessions in 1995, I've been reading and reading, looking for some kind of similarity, conformation, or validation of the information that surfaced. In the book *The Message of the Sphinx* by Graham Hancock and Robert Bauval, I found references to a "stargate." Evidently ancient Egyptian texts refer to the area around Orion's belt as a stargate or *duat*. Hancock and Bauval believe that the three stars in Orion's belt were so important that the ancient Egyptians positioned the three great pyramids in the same angular position as Orion's belt stars. Upon death, the pharaoh's soul was to pass through this stargate, which also functioned as a sort of time gate, because on the other side, the pharaoh could become immortal.

It sounded very much like the Star Gate in my hypnosis sessions. It was a place in the sky. It was a gate. And, on the other side, the soul was free and didn't know death. I remembered a time in the 1980s when I was assigned to do articles on the construction of a radio telescope at Kitt Peak, Arizona. At the time, I was fascinated with the constellation Orion, taking many photographs of "the hunter" above the telescopes. I did not know anything about the Egyptian duat at the time, but later learned of it from *The Message of the Sphinx*, published in 1996. Now I wonder if—on an unconscious level—I recognized Orion as the location for the Star Gate.

According to Hancock and Bauval's book, the builders of this ancient monument further emphasized Orion by pointing the Sphinx at the constellation Leo, is celestial counterpart. Leo rose around sunrise on the Spring Equinox during the years the Sphinx was being built. Above and ahead of Leo is Orion. It's as if the Sphinx is pointing to the Star Gate and the direction the pharaoh must travel to become immortal.

When We Were Gods

Recently, when I looked at star charts of the night sky, I was surprised to discover that behind Orion lies the star Arcturus. I wonder, then, if the builders of the Sphinx might be saying, "We became a creature that is stuck in the physical (half animal). Ahead of us and the way out is Orion. Behind us and the place we came from is Arcturus."

30

The Great Crystal

Originally appeared in
Circle Magazine:
Nature Spirituality Quarterly
Spring 2001, Issue 79
www.circlesanctuary.org/circle

The Circular room at the top of the tower was lit by a deep blue light. In the center of the room danced a little being that looked like a pixie-faced frog. Above her stood a giant spider, its eight legs anchored like columns along the perimeter of the room. The spider lovingly cradled something very precious in the folds of its white abdomen. It was the Great Crystal of Atlantis.

I had gone to a hypnotherapist for what we both considered would be routine sessions for weight reduction. Instead, I not only discovered past life reasons for my lifelong struggle with obesity, but also inadvertently stumbled upon my experiences in the long-lost, supposedly mythical, nation of Atlantis. This was all very well, except that in Atlantis I wasn't human. I was the pixie-faced little frog being.

The little frog's long sticky fingers held the top of an egg-shaped ball that floated in the blue light illuminating the round room. The indigo light was held in a white basin, similar to a present-day baptismal font. However, this basin floated in the air. A gold ring encircled both the bottom of the egg-shaped ball and the rim of the basin.

It turned out that the frog-being was controlling the Great Crystal. The egg-shaped ball pointed straight up at the Crystal held in the folds of the spider's abdomen. The Crystal produced energy by integrating gravity with the electromagnetic energy created by the relationship of the gold rings on the egg-shaped ball and the rim of the basin. Because the frog's pineal was open to gravitational and celestial energies, she could feel within her where the Sun was in relationship to the Moon and make the necessary adjustments.

Throughout this part of the Atlantis hypnosis session, my hand had continually moved on the arm of my chair as I adjusted the egg-shaped ball in my memory. When the hypnotherapist asked me what would happen if I stopped moving the ball, I answered as if it should be obvious, "We'd lose power." The Atlanteans used the power to levitate and rejuvenate.

According to America's best-documented psychic, Edgar Cayce, unscrupulous power-hungry elements of the Atlantean population eventually took control of the Crystal energy and tuned it too high, causing volcanic activity and the ultimate destruction of the great island nation.

In reading 519-001, Cayce refers to the Crystal as "the mighty, terrible crystal." He also called it a firestone in reading 440-5 and described it as "a large cylindrical glass . . . cut with facets in such a manner that the capstone on the top of same made for the centralizing of the power or force that concentrated between the end of the cylinder and the capstone itself." In addition, he said that records illustrating its construction could be found in three places in the Earth: in the sunken portions of Atlantis, in Egypt close to the Sphinx, and in the Mexican Yucatan.

I saw the Crystal as a green-glowing stone similar to an emerald. It was held by the spider just under the apex of the domed ceiling of the circular room, which was located at the top of a tall tower. The little frog-being kept her long-fingered hand on the floating ball directly under the spider's body, fine-tuning the adjustments that unified gravity with electromagnetism. The tower hummed.

Today we would make a machine. But in Atlantis we were very different beings than we are today. It took me a long time to understand what I was experiencing. Although I was open to the concept of reincarnation, I expected that in my previous lives I would have been a human being, not some strange pixie-faced animal. At first I was sure I was suffering from an overactive imagination. However, further research into the Cayce readings revealed what Cayce referred to as the root races.

According to Cayce, we were all originally Light Beings, capable of traversing the stars, making us truly citizens of the universe. When we became trapped in the physical, we were at first only a thought form. As we became more enmeshed in matter, as in Atlantis, we played with the physical by going in and out of previously existing naturally evolving entities, sometimes changing them (the pixie-face). I found similar information in *The Secret Doctrine* by Mme. Helene Blavatsky, and believe that the Maya and Hopi referred to the root races when they described previous worlds.

When the hypnotherapist asked me to go to the next important thing, I saw something like a pie shape open up, and I moved out of the frog-being and into the light. The hypnotherapist asked if, in my Atlantean memory, I had made the transition to the other side. I said, "No," because we didn't die at that time. My light essence had merely disengaged from the frog to rest and rejuvenate for awhile.

In Atlantis, we worked *in agreement with* nature. It was more like dancing with nature spirits. The spider, crystal, gold stripes, and frog were all part of the natural world, each with its innate characteristics. The spider could stand endlessly, the crystal could refract waves, the gold was a great microelectronic conductor, and the frog, with its sticky fingers and scalp-top pineal, was perfect for manipulating the floating egg-shaped ball in the gravitational field.

It was as if our semi-solid light bodies could enmesh with forces in the natural world.

Today we deal so much more harshly with nature. For example, we force minerals to become metals and force plants to produce more with unbalanced, unnatural fertilizers. However, in Atlantis, our work with the Great Crystal had originally been very loving and very much in agreement with the natural world. It was when we started forcing physical elements to produce more than they comfortably could that the trouble started.

In the hypnosis session, I was also told that our present-day human body operated on the same principle as the power source in Atlantis. Evidently the pineal gland in our bodies acts like the Crystal in the tower and integrates celestial influences with the electromagnetic energy of our body. We receive the celestial influences as sunlight through our eyes.

I was told that, as an expression of reverence to those natural laws, it would be valuable for all of us to greet the Sun every morning as it rises over the horizon. In that way, we could reset our body rhythms as they were meant to be. Just like the Great Crystal, our own crystal/pineal needs to be managed lovingly and in agreement with the natural world.

31

Searching for the Hall of Records in the Yucatan

Originally appeared in
Venture Inward
March/April 2001, Volume 17 Number 2
www.edgarcayce.org/venture_inward

Many A.R.E. members know about the search for the Hall of Records that has been going on in Egypt for many years. Fewer may be aware that there evidently is another place where Atlantean archives are buried. In reading 440-5 Cayce says that the records from the fabled Lost Continent are not only in the temple records of Egypt, but were also carried to Yucatan.

According to 5750-1, "The records are one." They contain "a record of Atlantis from the beginnings of those periods when the spirit took form or began the encasements in that land . . ." (378-16) They extend through the first destructions of that ancient civilization, the exodus of Atlanteans to other lands, and the final destruction of Atlantis. They contain a description of the building of the Great Pyramid, as well as a prophecy of "who, what, where, would come [to make] the opening of the records . . ." (378-16)

When We Were Gods

Perennially fascinated with Atlantis and unwilling to join the hordes flocking to the right forepaw of the Sphinx, my husband and I journeyed to the Yucatan to see what we might find. While the readings on the Yucatan Hall of Records are not as specific as those on Egypt, they contain many clues. Therefore, clutching the Hall of Records readings in our eager hands, we flew to Cancun, on Mexico's Yucatan peninsula, and began our search.

We were looking for something that "might be termed the sundial that lies between the temple and the chambers." (440-12) I felt that the temple we were searching for might be a pyramid because reading 2329-3 uses the word "temple" interchangeably with "pyramid." Moreover, since the Egyptian Hall of Records is thought to be close to the Great Pyramid, it seemed probable that its Yucatan counterpart would likely be close to a pyramid as well.

There are many Mayan pyramids in Guatemala, Honduras, and Mexico, especially close to Mexico City and in the Yucatan. However, Cayce located this Hall of Records in Yucatan, so we restricted our search to that region. As we traveled the paved and sometimes pot-holed roads slicing through the Mexican jungle, we wondered if the temple or pyramid we hoped to discover was still engulfed by vegetation and unknown to modern man, similar to the extensive ruins in Coba which have only recently been found and are still in the process of being unearthed and repaired.

However, we were encouraged by reading 440-5, which said that "the records that were carried to what is now Yucatan in America . . . are now . . . being uncovered." That reading was given in December 1933. Therefore, we assumed that the place we were looking for was open to the public by now. We hoped that one of the major Mayan ruins on the Yucatan peninsula—Tulum, Chichen Itza, or Uxmal—might be our destination.

Tulum, our first stop, was gorgeous. The main temple was perched like a citadel on a cliff overlooking the azure Caribbean. But there were no pyramids and we saw no sundial. In addition, although Tulum is part of the Yucatan peninsula, it is in the state of Quintana Roo rather than in Yucatan. Since Cayce in trance was often very specific, we thought that when he said "what is now Yucatan" he probably meant specifically in the state of Yucatan.

Therefore we headed inland toward Chichen Itza, a beautifully excavated and restored ruin that is famous for the snake sculptures that flank the stairway leading to the top of its main pyramid. At the spring equinox, sunlight falls along the stairs in such a way that it appears that a snake undulates up the stairway. Chichen Itza, with its observatory, snake carvings, temples, and pyramids, contains endless opportunities for exploration. However, we didn't find a sundial.

We decided to head off the beaten tourist path along goat-crossed roads flanked by Mayan communities to Izamal, nicknamed Ciudad Amarillo (Yellow City) because of its picturesque buildings. Although the town is a disappointment as an archeological site—its one pyramid rises in the middle of a village like a huge uninhabited hill (without any sundial)—Izamal is known for its church, which was visited by Pope John Paul II in 1993. It is dedicated to the Virgin of the Immaculate Conception, patron saint of the Yucatan.

Continuing our search for the Hall of Records, we journeyed toward Uxmal, arriving in town well after nightfall. Our headlights glared over narrow streets which wound, forked, twisted, and seemed to end up in the same spot over and over again. We bumped along in the dust past dwelling places, a church, and open garages illuminated by one incandescent light. Around us passed shadowy forms on motorcycles, in vehicles, and on foot, speaking with animation to each other in words that in no way resembled English.

We remembered all the admonitions from home, "Never drive in Mexico after dark!" and wondered what fate might befall us. "Uxmal?" my husband shouted out to a group of three men by the side of the road. One of the group came over to my husband's window and carefully, sincerely, and with honest concern showed us, with hand signs lit by refracted light from our headlights, and very slow Spanish, which roads to take. Somehow my husband understood him. Within an hour we had found Uxmal and were gratefully settled in our motel room. Despite all the warnings, our many encounters with the Mexican people proved friendly and helpful.

Uxmal was an especially important destination, and not only because of the Cayce readings. I had also read in *The World Before* that Ruth Montgomery, best-selling author on the paranormal, said that her "spirit guides" had revealed the Uxmal vicinity as the location of the Yucatan Hall of Records.

In addition, when Cayce was asked how the Great Pyramid was built, he had answered, "By the use of those forces in nature as make for iron to swim. Stone floats in the air in the same manner." (5748-6) Since the Great Pyramid, which he said is close to the Egyptian Hall of Records, was built by an exceptional method, I wondered if the temple beside the Yucatan Hall of Records might also have been built in an unusual way. Moreover, in reading 5750-1 on the Yucatan, Cayce was asked, "By what power or powers were these early pyramids and temples constructed?" He replied, "By the lifting forces of those gases . . ."

One of our guidebooks mentioned an extraordinary legend about Uxmal's main pyramid. It had evidently been "built by a magician in one night." That clue made me think this might be the place.

It sounded very much like my past-life memories of the construction of the Great Pyramid. In past-life regressions, I had inadvertently stumbled upon my own experiences in Atlantis, including memories of the building of the Great Pyramid. It wasn't by dragging 20-ton boulders up earthen ramps on oiled skids. I had seen huge stone blocks flying through the air. The flying stones had not just hovered. They had zinged through the air so fast that they blurred as they dematerialized and rematerialized into the exactly correct spot. It seemed likely, then, that a pyramid with the reputation of having been built in a single night would have been built by Atlanteans.

That's why I really wanted to see the Pyramid of the Sorcerer in Uxmal. By chance, this pyramid happened to be built right beside a three-foot tall column that our guide referred to as a sundial.

Consulting the Cayce information, I read that the temple in the Yucatan is "overshadowing" the Hall of Records. (2012-1) My first view of the sundial was in the early morning while it was overshadowed by the Pyramid of the Sorcerer. I stood in the middle of an archway that perfectly framed the sundial and waited while the sun rose, freeing the sundial of the shade. Behind it, the main stairway of the Pyramid of the Sorcerer ascended to a temple faced with Chaac, the rain god, whose fierce countenance glowered down as if in warning and protection, but of what—a sundial?

Opposite the Pyramid of the Sorcerer, on the other side of the sundial, is a square called the Quadrangle of the Nuns, because it is lined with cells that look like the small rooms found in a nunnery. I remembered 440-12 " . . . the sundial that lies between the temple and the chambers." This Yucatan relic is called a sundial, is between a temple and chambers, and is overshadowed by the temple on top of the pyramid. I wondered, could the Hall of Records be nearby?

Other researchers have different ideas of where this legendary repository may be found. Lora Little and John Van Auken, authors of a new book, *The Lost Hall of Records: Edgar Cayce's Forgotten Record of Human History in the Ancient Yucatan,* concluded that the Hall of Records in the western hemisphere is in Guatemala at Piedras Negras, which is situated along the Usumacinta River border with Mexico. They base this on a different interpretation of the Cayce readings.

I had interpreted the Cayce readings to mean that the search for the Hall of Records would best be confined to the Mexican province of Yucatan. Other inquiring minds had felt that Cayce could have meant areas on the Yucatan peninsula beyond the Mexican province of that name, including neighboring Guatemala.

In a telephone interview, Lora Little said that she had found 17 clues in the Cayce readings suggesting the location of the Atlantean information. However, just as I honed in on specific clues, Little also focused her fact finding attention on specific clues in the readings.

For example, in 440-5, the December 1933 reading mentioned above, Cayce said that "these stones are now—during the last few months—being uncovered." The stones Cayce referred to were associated with the crystal "firestone" that was used by the Atlanteans for power. Evidently the records describing the firestone's construction were also in the Hall of Records. Further along in reading 440-5, Cayce says that an emblem representing the stones would be carried to the Pennsylvania State Museum.

Unfortunately, there is no museum called specifically the "Pennsylvania State Museum." Dr. Little conducted an extensive search through archives of state-funded museums in Pennsylvania to discover which, if any, contained stones unearthed in the Yucatan area in 1933. She found that the State Museum of Pennsylvania, which is associated with the University of Pennsylvania, had records that revealed that the only archeological work undertaken in the Yucatan area during 1933 had occurred at Piedras Negras in Guatemala. She was heartened to learn that Brigham Young University has been in the same location as well, looking for evidence of the Lost Tribes of Israel. Like Cayce, Brigham Young believed the Lost Tribes had been in the Americas.

John Van Auken, who is also a former executive director of A.R.E., says that there are three caves in Piedras Negras that are very likely candidates for the location of the Hall of Records. However, neither he nor Dr. Little have explored the site. Piedras Negras can only be reached by canoe, including portages through treacherous tropical jungle. Not only must all food and water be brought in, but even water for bathing has to be transported due to the risk of infection from the river. "I'm not a hardship kind of guy," says Van Auken.

My husband and I are not the only ones who have gone looking for the Yucatan Hall of Records. Scott Milburn, a Virginia Beach videographer, reported to the A.R.E. Congress last June on his journeys down the Usumacinta River just over the border in Guatemala. He has explored the ancient Mayan site of Y-Okib, meaning the "entrance" or "cave," now called Piedras Negras on three occasions. In the process of making a documentary, he plans to return to Guatemala in April and will lead an A.R.E. tour to Mayan sites in Mexico in May.

Thus far, however, like the elusive chamber beneath the Sphinx in Egypt, the location of the Atlantean records in the West remains as mysterious as their contents.

32

The Man of My Dreams

Originally appeared in
*Dream Network: A Journal
Exploring Dreams & Mythology*
Autumn 2001, Volume 20 No. 8
www.dreamnetwork.net

Because I met my husband first in a dream people are always asking me how to find the man or woman of their dreams.

I'm afraid it's not that easy. Dreams come out of the wild, untamed infinity of the unconscious mind which cannot be controlled in the same way we go after a goal in the physical world. Nonetheless, I would like to share with you some of the ways I've learned how to dance with the unconscious so that I receive guidance and insight in my dreams.

The unconscious needs to be welcomed. It needs to know that you like dancing with it and that you'd like to meet it—your very own special unconscious with all its complexes, karmic memories, and biases.

Most books on working with dreams recommend that you keep a dream journal by your bed with a pen at the ready. As soon as you awaken, write your dreams down before they slip away into the clacking of the day. To show your unconscious your willingness to dance, it's also a good idea to record your dreams even if you awaken in the middle of the night. If you share your bedroom with other people and don't want to wake them by turning on the light, keep a flashlight by the bed.

But, you say, "I don't remember my dreams." That's O.K. Even people who easily remember dreams don't remember them every single night. Begin by noting how you feel as you wake up. Write it down. Reading books on dreaming also helps as does talking about dreams . . . anything that sets your consciousness compass toward dream recall.

Once you're remembering dreams and writing them down, you can begin to notice what symbols your particular unconscious uses and what they mean to you. Most dreams are symbolically about the dreamer. Working with dreams means learning about yourself.

For example, if a dog bit you when you were a child, likely dreaming of a dog will mean something entirely different to you than it will to the person whose endearing comfort as a youngster was a big, smelly, loving, faithful beast. As you sort out your own symbols, your unconscious will see that you have come to the dance and are standing on the dance floor waiting for a partner.

There are also many books with lists of dream symbols to quicken your associations. It also helps to look back in your journal over your dreams from about a month ago. Suddenly they make sense in light of how your life is progressing.

Besides cataloging my own personal dream symbols, I have found that my dreams often use words in clever ways. For example, the day before I'd dreamed of the man I would marry, I'd had my last date with a man who had proposed marriage to me. Although this man was a multi-millionaire and I was a struggling single mom with three children, I'd declined his proposal, because I didn't love the man. In the dream, the man I should marry was first represented by the actor Godonuv. I realized that the dream had meant that this man may not be a milti-millionaire, but he was, nonetheless, "Godonov" or "good enough" for me.

236

Article: The Man of My Dreams

However, to really dance with the unconscious, you need to do more than remember, record, and understand your dreams. You need to be willing to follow suggestions you've been given, always weighing the information by your innate common sense. In your awake life, you wouldn't jump off a bridge just because someone told you to. So too with dreams.

Therefore, after you've ascertained the suggestions given in your dreams are not harmful to you or anyone else, you can show your unconscious that you're humming the music by following up on your dream suggestions. During the search for my twin soul, I dreamt that I would find him, a man named Ian Finlayson, on the walkway over Toronto City Hall's skating rink.

At the time, I lived in Phoenix, Arizona. However, a year later, when I found myself in Toronto, my children cringed in embarrassment as I watched the men pass me on the overhead walkway, hoping for some sense of recognition and trying to muster my courage to ask, "Are you Ian Finlayson?" My courage never mustered. Nonetheless, I did call all the Finlayson's in the Toronto Phone Book and ask, "Is Ian there?" He wasn't.

Although this sounds crazy, it is entertaining, takes courage, and, to my mind, is no less insane than spending the evening watching stock cars crashing into themselves or mutilating parts of the body by piercing ears (myself included), tongues, bellybuttons, breasts, and penises. The only difference is that millions of people watch stock car races and pierce holes in their bodies, while only a very few are doing the hard work of learning how to unlock the great potential of their unconscious minds.

The reality is that working with dreams is somewhat like living by the rules of fairy tales. You have to be willing to do the silly tasks, like carrying the Golden Goose, to be able to win the hand of the princess. There are tests.

There is a reason for the tests. It's like a friend coming up to you on the dance floor and saying, "Do you see that tall, dark, handsome stranger over there?"

And you answer, voice a-quiver, "Yes?"

"Well, if he asked you, would you dance with him?"

You have to be willing to dance with him. After all, if I was willing to stand on the overhead walkway at Toronto City Hall, perhaps, if I was given a dream that told me a certain man was "Godonuv" for me, and then the dream showed me his house, his dog, his best friend, and his work, as well as the man smiling in front of me, perhaps when I saw him the next day, I might have the guts to go up to him an say "Hello."

Unfortunately, despite my Ian Finlayson test, when I did see the man I had dreamt about, I almost fainted. For me, it took a year before I had the strength to approach the man of my dreams. In the meanwhile, I dated every other guy who asked me.

I was afraid. But, what was I afraid of? Although we may want to work with the power of the unconscious, when it actually begins asking us to dance, i.e. cooperating with us, the great fear is that it will take us over. What scares the pants off us is that to dance with the unconscious requires that we let it lead. I feared that I might have a destiny. And I did. It's all in the book I wrote about my experiences: *When We Were Gods: Insights on Atlantis, Past Lives, Angelic Beings of Light, and Spiritual Awakening.*

However, you don't only have to use your dreams to find your soul mate. You can also work with your unconscious to raise your children, find your right career, make a better home, travel, improve relationships, and also connect with the spiritual.

Then one day, after working with your dreams for a while, you will dream that the reason why your baby is having trouble sleeping is that he's cutting a molar. You will assume that images are symbolic and will write the dream down in you journal with all the others, noting that for you dreams of babies usually mean new beginnings. You will consult your list of dream symbols for emerging teeth. Perhaps you'll look up molars and teeth in a dream book. Then, just for fun, you'll look in your baby's mouth and low and behold, you'll see a big red lump in his gums.

That's when you'll know that you're on the dance floor whirling to the music: when the unconscious is not only working in symbols but also giving you direct knowledge about your life. Then you're well on your way to integrating the power of the unconscious with

Article: The Man of My Dreams

your conscious life. And someday, you just may dream about the man you should marry. Good Luck.

33

In the Mouth of the Snake

Originally appeared in
Alternate Perceptions
February 2002, Issue 53
www.mysterious-america.net

In February 1999, my husband and I traveled to Yucatan in Mexico to look for evidence of some unusual information I'd received in past life regressions on Atlantis. While under trance I had seen myself fall into the mouth of a huge snake. Immediately afterward, I'd flown through space over Atlantis and had landed in what is now Egypt where the Great Pyramid was under construction. This memory of falling into the snake's mouth was the most challenging of my recollections in past life regression.

In 1995, four years before my trip to Yucatan, I had entered a hypnotherapist's office with the expectation of some routine sessions on weight loss. Because I'd been struggling with weight my whole life, the therapist suggested I go back to the "karmic causative factor"—basically to search for the original reason in my past that had caused my spirit to create obesity in my body.

To both our surprise, I first went to an experience in which I wasn't even human. I found myself to be a pure Light Being from

Arcturus who had become trapped in the physical on Earth. However, my first material body wasn't human either. I was more like a thought form that I experienced as a wisp-of-smoke almost like a genie in a lamp. It turned out that the reason for my obesity was to remind myself of the weight of the physical so I would search to be free and go "home." I had to admit that throughout my life I had been constantly searching, from studying the Cayce readings to researching the mystery of the Great Pyramid.

Although I am presently writing the above with composure, I can assure you that at the time of the hypnosis sessions I was shocked to learn that I appeared to be an alien trapped in the Earth. Until that time, although I had a voracious interest in the paranormal, it had for the most part been as an observer rather than a participant. I had read about past life regressions, in which other people had discovered they were originally from other star systems, for example, in Dick Sutphen's books. Such readings eventually allowed me to accept the idea of being from Arcturus. I was also able to accept some of my experiences in Atlantis because of my previous exploration.

To begin, I found myself to be three beings all at the same time: 1. a pixie-faced frog that controlled the Atlantean power source, the Great Crystal; 2. a scientist who had developed the Crystal technology; and 3. a woman with a small child. As hypnosis sessions progressed, I began to recognize that I was experiencing the root races that Edgar Cayce in his readings and Madame Blavatsky in *The Secret Doctrine* had described.

Evidently, we were all at one time citizens of the universe capable of traversing star systems. According to Kirk Nelson in his 1994 *Venture Inward* article, "The Fifth Root Race," the four root races according to Cayce were "spirit, thought form, projection into matter, and Adamic man or Homo Sapiens." Therefore, by reading about the root races I was able to understand the unusual concept of "projection into matter" in three simultaneous bodies, as I found myself to be in Atlantis. In fact, I wondered if I had imagined the root races because I had previously read about them.

Nonetheless, the next part of the Atlantis session stretched even my ability to embrace the unusual memories I was experiencing, probably because I had never seen anything in print about my experiences. When the hypnotherapist asked me to go to the next significant event, I saw myself fall into the mouth of a huge snake. It appeared as if the earth below me formed itself into a gigantic snake's mouth. I could even see the fangs in the upper jaw. I told the therapist that we had to be trusting and a "letting go" kind of people. It was as if I had disengaged myself from the three animals I had been merged with: the pixie-faced frog, the Atlantean scientist, and the mother—and became my essence, which I described as a "semi-solid encapsulated" Light Being. This essence fell into the snake's mouth.

Next, I saw myself as a spinning glowing ball speeding through space. Below me stretched Atlantis in the first throes of earth upheavals. When I landed, I was in Egypt at the site of the Great Pyramid, which was surrounded by green grass with water nearby. The hypnotherapist kept asking me questions trying to clarify what I was seeing. Over and over, I re-experienced the memory of falling into the snake's mouth and speeding through space to land in Egypt. Suddenly, I realized that I was reliving an experience of working in agreement with nature. Through this agreement I could merge my light essence with previously existing natural beings, for example, the mother and the Atlantean scientist. In addition, again through an agreement with nature, I could alter the previously existing natural objects, for example, by creating a pixie-faced frog rather than a normal-faced frog.

It is hard for us to comprehend the type of powerful beings we were in Atlantis. Because we presently inhabit only one body at a time—the one we're born with—and usually only go out of it when we are unconscious (e.g., when we are asleep or drugged or during a near death experience) it is very difficult to conceive of anything different from our selves, especially that our souls would have the capability to inhabit numerous bodies simultaneously and to enter and leave at will. Although many of us are learning how to work with the energies of our bodies to heal ourselves, no one I know can change their body as radically as creating a pixie-face on a frog. And, these changes were accomplished gently and in agreement with nature rather than the changes we can now force through manufacturing processes, with surgery, or genetic manipulation.

In addition, we merged with the various animal or mineral elements because of their innate characteristics. For example, it appeared that I had fallen into the snake's mouth to use the snake's strike capability to propel my "semi-solid encapsulated" body to safety in Egypt. Again, it appears that I am writing these words with equanimity, but at the time I was so challenged by the image of falling into the snake's mouth, I felt that I must be crazy to believe it. I needed validation that these images existed somewhere else than in my mind.

Therefore, I had to go to the Yucatan. I had read that many Mayan ruins contained stone carvings of men in the mouths of feathered serpents. However, the explanation for these unusual images were all theories—that the stone carvings represented kundalini, a snake cult, etc.—all guesses. I realized that no one really knows why the ancient Maya seemed to be fascinated with images of men in snake's mouths. I wondered if perhaps my past life regressions had shed some light on an ancient mystery.

I suspected that, based on my Atlantean memories, the ancient Maya had reconstructed their memories of Atlanteans traveling via snake transportation by making their snakes feathered, e.g., snakes that could fly like birds. The Third Root Race Atlanteans had to fall into the snake's mouth in order to merge with the snake. I also suspected that the Atlanteans used the snake's strike capability to propel the "semi-solid encapsulated" light body to fly to its destination.

My husband and I had read in Peter Tompkin's *Mysteries of the Mexican Pyramids* that most of the stone images of feathered serpents now reposed in museums. Would we find one in its original location? Fortunately, in Uxmal our search produced results. The guide pointed me to the east facing wall of the Nunnery Quadrangle. There I found a feathered serpent whose body undulated along the wall and pointed to a panel containing images of the planet Venus. In the snake's mouth was a man's face.

I can't tell you the immense relief I felt upon seeing that image. Here was a snake that was carrying a man through space past Venus. This was exactly my experience in Atlantis. The snake had carried me (as a semi-solid encapsulated body) through space to land in Egypt.

In Tulum, I also saw an engraving of a man falling head first. This image is called, "The Descending God." It looked exactly like my memory of falling headfirst into the snake's mouth.

During our travels in Yucatan, my husband and I had the good fortune to meet Hilario Hilaire, an American who had lived in a Mayan village for ten years, most of it married to a Mayan woman. Hilario describes himself as an amateur archeologist and professional tour guide. We happened to stay in Akumal just down the street from Hilario's apartment.

Because of my interest in the ancient Maya, I asked Hilario if I could interview him. I was delighted when he agreed. While we talked, I was wondering if it would be appropriate to mention my Atlantean memories of snake transportation. I started by discussing the many images of men in snake's mouths that had been found in the Yucatan. Before I got to mention my Atlantean experience, Hilario volunteered that in his experience with Mayan shamans, they had said that if ever a person has a dream or vision of coming out of a snake's mouth, the next thing they would see is the truth.

In my hypnosis sessions, the next thing that happened after emerging from the snake's mouth and landing in Egypt was a vision telling me that it was my purpose in this lifetime to awaken the "Golden Ones," souls who had taken on the task in Atlantis to reincarnate now and bring in a new world. I was to write a book or in some way through mass media inform them of the history of the soul through the root races. These Golden Ones would survive the coming earth changes to bring forth a new type of physical being, the Fifth Root Race. Unlike the Atlanteans who were motivated by power, the Fifth Root Race would be motivated by love.

My experience has led me to write a book. It is now called, *When We Were Gods: Insights on Atlantis, Past Lives, Angelic Beings of Light, and Spiritual Awakening.* The original edition was published by CPS in May 2001. (The book is currently published by SunTopaz.)

While writing the book, I was also amazed to discover that there were images in Egypt of snakes transporting people in the sky. Many of these images can be found in The Book of What is in the Duat in the tombs of Amenhotep II and Tuthmosis III.

In September 2000, I traveled to Luxor, Egypt, with Peggy Rose Day, my CPS publisher, to explore and photograph snake transportation images in the tombs of the pharaohs. We were amazed at the number of paintings we found of snakes with wings, with feet, in the shape of boats, and with Egyptians sitting on them as if riding on a carriage—one image after another of snakes used for transportation. There were also many images from the Egyptian Book of the Gates, which depict gates with a snake standing on its tail along the middle of the gate. It was as if the gate between one place and another is traversed via a snake.

In addition, the ancient Egyptians were often drawn with the heads of animals, which reminded me of my Third Root Race experience in Atlantis when I had the ability to take on animal forms. We found that the Egyptian gods were portrayed as sun discs. The sun discs reminded me of how I'd reverted to my "semi-solid encapsulated" light body essence when I'd separated myself from the animal bodies in Atlantis. In trance, I had described myself as looking like a glowing cannonball spinning through space.

Probably our most significant discovery was in the tomb of Tuthmosis III. There, painted across the width of the ceiling, a sun disc flies through the stars supported by giant wings led by two snake heads. According to Webster's dictionary, this sun disc represents Ra, the Egyptian sun god. To me the sun disc also represented the "semi-solid encapsulated" light body flying (the wings) through space (the stars) by snake power (the snake heads).

Article: In the Mouth of the Snake

The Cayce readings say that when earth upheavals began to break up Atlantis, the Atlanteans immigrated to safety lands in the Yucatan and Egypt. I believe the Yucatan stone carvings of feathered serpents with men in their mouths and winged, footed, etc. snakes in Egypt are records of that exodus. In their artwork, the ancient Egyptians and Maya immortalized their memories of the Third Root Race Atlantean abilities. In addition, I believe that the pharaoh's Book of What is in the Duat was partially written to establish the pharaohs as direct descendants of the "gods" from Atlantis as well as to describe our journey through the root races.

Based on my visits to Yucatan and Egypt, I believe we need to consider that the creators of images of men in the mouths of feathered serpents and snakes with wings and feet truly represent an actual event in our soul's history. These images are an attempt to visually convey that which we no longer experience—the time when we were still "semi-solid encapsulated" Light Beings. It was a time when we could go into and out of previously existing animals, including the ability to use snakes to provide instant transportation.

Bibliography

Arguelles, Jose, Ph.D. *The Mayan Factor: Path Beyond Technology*. Santa Fe: Bear & Company Publishing, 1987.

Assaad, Hany, and Daniel Kolos. *The Name of the Dead: Tutankhamun Translated*. Mississauga, Ontario, Canada: Benben Publications, 1979.

Auken, John van, and Lora H. Little. *The Lost Hall of Records: Edgar Cayce's Forgotten Record of Human History in the Ancient Yucatan*. Memphis: Eagle Wing Books, 2000.

Blavatsky, H. P. *The Secret Doctrine: The Synthesis of Science, Religion, and Philosophy, Volumes I and II*. Los Angeles: The Theosophy Company, 1888.

Carroll, Lee, and Jan Tober. *The Indigo Children: The New Kids Have Arrived*. Flagstaff, AZ: Light Technology Publications, 1999.

Castaneda, Carlos. *The Teachings of Don Juan: A Yaqui Way of Knowledge*. New York: Pocket Books, 1968.

Cayce, Edgar Evans. *Edgar Cayce on Atlantis*. New York: Paperback Library, 1968.

Cayce, Edgar Evans, Gail Cayce Schwartzer, and Douglas G. Richards. *Mysteries of Atlantis Revisited: An Edgar Cayce Guide*. New York: St. Martin's Paperbacks, 1988.

Cerminara, Gina. *Many Mansions: The Edgar Cayce Story on Reincarnation*. New York: A Signet Book, 1967.

Collins, Andrew. *Gateway to Atlantis: The Search for the Source of a Lost Civilization*. New York: Carroll & Graf Publishers, 2002.

Corson, Col. Philip J. (Ret.), with William J. Birnes. *The Day After Roswell: A Former Pentagon Official Reveals the U.S. Government's Shocking UFO Cover-up*. New York: Pocket Books, 1997.

Cotterell, Maurice M. *The Supergods: They Came on a Mission to Save Mankind*. London: HarperCollins, 1997.

Day, Peggy Rose, and Susan Gale. *Edgar Cayce on the Indigo Children*. Virginia Beach: A.R.E. Press, 2004.

Dosick, Wayne, and Ellen Kaufman. *Spiritually Healing the Indigo Children (and Adult Indigos, too!): The Practical Guide and Handbook*. San Diego: Jodere Group, 2004.

Dunn, Christopher. *Giza Power Plant: Technologies of Ancient Egypt*. Santa Fe: Bear & Company Publishing, 1988.

Findhorn Community. *The Findhorn Garden: Pioneering a New Vision of Man and Nature in Cooperation*. New York: Harper & Row, 1968.

Frissell, Bob. *Nothing in This Book is True But It Is Exactly The Way Things Are: The Esoteric Meanings of the Monuments on Mars*. Berkeley: Frog Ltd, 2003.

Bibliography

Grant, Robert J. *Are We Listening to the Angels: The Next Step in Understanding Angels in Our Lives.* Virginia Beach: A.R.E. Press, 1994.

Hancock, Graham. *Fingerprints of the Gods: The Evidence of Earth's Lost Civilization.* New York: Three Rivers Press, 1996.

Hancock, Graham, and Robert Bauval. *The Message of the Sphinx: A Quest for the Hidden Legacy of Mankind.* New York: Three Rivers Press, 1997.

Hancock, Graham and Santha Faiia. *Heaven's Mirror: Quest for the Lost Civilization.* New York: Three Rivers Press, 1998.

Hapgood, Charles H. *The Earth's Shifting Crust: A Key to Some Basic Problems of Earth Science.* New York: Pantheon Books, 1969.

Hapgood, Charles H. *The Path of the Pole.* Philadelphia: Chilton Book Company, 1970.

Joudry, Patricia, and Maurie D. Pressman, M.D. *Twin Souls: Finding Your True Spiritual Partner.* Center City, MN: Hazelden Publishing & Educational Services, September, 2000.

Kime, Zane R., M.D., M.S. *Sunlight.* Penryn, CA: World Health Publications, 1980.

Laughton, Timothy. *The Maya: Life, Myth, and Art.* New York: Stewart, Tabori, and Chang, 1998.

Liberman, Jacob, O.D., Ph.D. *Light: Medicine of the Future.* Santa Fe: Bear & Company Publishing, 1991.

Mack, John E. *Abductions: Human Encounters with Aliens.* New York: Ballantine Books, 1995.

MacLaine, Shirley. *The Camino: A Journey of the Spirit.* New York: Pocket Books, 2000.

MacLean, Dorothy. *To Hear the Angels Sing: An Odyssey of Co-creation with the Devic Kingdom.* Barrington, MA: Lindisfarne Books, 1994.

Mellin, Laurel, M.A., R.D. *The Solution: Six Winning Ways to Permanent Weight Loss.* New York: HarperPerennial, 1998.

Moody, Raymond, M.D., with Paul Perry. *Reunions: Visionary Encounters with Departed Loved Ones.* New York: Villard Books, 1993.

Montgomery, Ruth. *Aliens Among Us.* New York: Putnam, 1985.

Montgomery, Ruth. *The World Before: Arthur Ford and the Great Guides reveal Earth's Secret Past and Future.* New York: A Fawcett Crest Book, 1976.

Montgomery, Ruth. *The World to Come: The Guides' Long Awaited Predictions for the Dawning Age.* New York: Harmony Books, 1999.

Morgan, Marlo. *Mutant Message Down Under.* New York: HarperPerennial, 1994.

Nelson, Kirk. *The Second Coming.* Virginia Beach: Wright Publishing Company, 1992.

Newton, Michael, Ph.D. *Destiny of Souls: New Case Studies of Life Between Lives.* St. Paul: Llewellyn Publications, 2001.

Bibliography

Pereira, Patricia L. *Songs of the Arcturians: The Arcturian Star Chronicles, Volume I*. Hillsboro, OR: Beyond Word Publishing, 1996.

Prophet, Elizabeth Clare. *Soul Mates and Twin Flames: The Spiritual Dimension of Love and Relationships*. Corwin Springs, MT: Summit University Press, 1999.

Renard, Gary R. *The Disappearance of the Universe: Straight Talk About Illusions, Past Lives, Religion, Sex, Politics and the Miracles of Forgiveness*. Carlsbad, CA: Hay House, 2002.

Sanderfur, Glenn. *Lives of the Master: The Rest of the Jesus Story*. Virginia Beach: A.R.E. Press, 1988.

Smith, A. Robert, Ed. *The Lost Memoirs of Edgar Cayce: Life as a Seer*. Virginia Beach: A.R.E. Press, 1997.

Steiner, Rudolf. *Atlantis and Lemuria*. Mokelumne Hill, CA: Health Research, 1963.

Stern, Jess. *Edgar Cayce on the Millennium: The Famed Prophet Visualizes a Bright New World*. New York: Warner Books, 1998.

Stern, Jess. *Soul Mates*. New York: Bantam, 1984.

Strieber, Whitley. *Communion: A True Story*. New York: Avon Books, 1988.

Sugrue, Thomas. *There is a River: The Story of Edgar Cayce*. Virginia Beach: A.R.E. Press, 1945.

Sutphen, Dick. *Past Lives, Future Loves*. New York: Pocket, 1990.

Taylor, Robert. *What the Bible Says About the End Times: Prophecies You Can't Ignore*. Bacon Raton, FL: Globe Digests, 2001.

Thurston, Mark, Ph.D. *Millennium Prophecies: Predictions for the Coming Century from Edgar Cayce*. New York: Kensington Books, 1997.

Tompkins, Peter. *Mysteries of the Mexican Pyramids*. New York: HarperCollins, 1987.

Tompkins, Peter. *Secrets of the Great Pyramid*. New York: Harper & Row, 1971.

Twyman, James. *Emissary of Love: The Psychic Children Speak to the World*. Charlottesville, VA: Hampton Roads Publishing, 2002

Velikovsky, Immanuel. *Earth in Upheaval*. Garden City, NY: Doubleday, 1955.

Velikovsky, Immanuel. *Worlds in Collision*. New York: Pocket, 1984.

Virtue, Doreen. *The Crystal Children: A Guide to the Newest Generation of Psychic and Sensitive Children*. Carlsbad, CA: Hay House, 2003.

Waters, Frank. *Mexico Mystique: The Coming Sixth World of Consciousness*. Chicago: Swallow Press, 1975.

West, John Anthony. *Serpent in the Sky: The High Wisdom of Ancient Egypt*. Wheaton, IL: Quest, 1993.

Bibliography

West, John Anthony. *The Traveler's Key to Ancient Egypt: A Guide to the Sacred places of Ancient Egypt.* Wheaton, IL: Quest Books, 1995.

Zukav, Gary. *The Seat of the Soul.* New York: A Fireside Book, Simon & Schuster, 1989.

Index

Index

Index

Author Biography

Carole Chapman is an internationally acclaimed author, speaker, and media personality. She enjoys publicizing her speaking events with radio interviews and book signings both in the United States and Canada.

Chapman's seminars are not only informative and transformational but also fun and entertaining. She always includes several workshops so the audience can participate.

A frequent guest on radio talk shows, Chapman has been featured on the Doug Stephan Show and Coast-to-Coast AM (Art Bell, now George Noory).

She is also an award-winning photographer. While a photojournalist under contract to NASA, her photographs appeared in publications throughout the world including *Koku-Fan* (Japan), *Aeronautique Astronautique* (France), *Aeronautica & Difesa* (Italy), *Air and Space Smithsonian, Aerospace America, Details,* and *Final Frontier.*

As a freelance writer and photographer, her illustrated articles have been published in *Sunset, Arizona Living, Dream Network, Circle, Alternate Perceptions, Phoenix Magazine, Fate, Whole Life Times,* and *Venture Inward.*

She studied photography and filmmaking at Ryerson University in Toronto and has a bachelor's degree in journalism from Prescott College.

Chapman and her husband love to travel. They live on a river in southeastern Virginia where they sail and keep a large organic garden.

Additional Copies of

When We Were Gods
(ISBN: 0-9754691-1-8)

may be purchased from

Amazon.com
BarnesandNoble.com
or your Local Book Seller

Visit the author's website at:
www.CaroleChapman.com

Do you have memories of Atlantis?
Or, memories of the root races?

Carole says, "*When We Were Gods* is the story of my memories of Atlantis. As I give my seminars throughout the USA and Canada, I come across people who also have memories of Atlantis or the root races. Therefore, I am collecting other people's stories for a future book. If it is responsive to you, please write to me with your own memories of Atlantis or the root races."

AtlantisMemories@CaroleChapman.com

For personal appearances and media requests, please
contact the Publicity Department at SunTopaz

publicity@SunTopaz.com

Printed in the United States
202773BV00003B/214-237/A